Co
Drive

a Wolters Kluwer business

Wolters Kluwer (UK) Limited
145 London Road
Kingston upon Thames
Surrey KT2 6SR
Tel: 020 8247 1175

Published by
Wolters Kluwer (UK) Limited
145 London Road
Kingston upon Thames
Surrey KT2 6SR
Tel: 020 8247 1175

First published December 1987
Second Edition 1989
Third Edition 1993
Fourth Edition 1997
Fifth Edition 2004
Sixth Edition 2005
Seventh Edition 2006
Eighth Edition 2007

© Wolters Kluwer (UK) Limited

All rights reserved. No part of this publication may be reproduced, stored in a retrieval system, or transmitted in any form or by any means, electronic, mechanical, photocopying, recording, or otherwise, without the prior permission of Wolters Kluwer (UK) Limited or the original copyright holder.

Crown copyright material is reproduced with the permission of the

Controller of HMSO and the Queen's Printer for Scotland. Although great care has been taken in the compilation and preparation of this book to ensure accuracy, the publishers cannot in any circumstances accept responsibility for any errors or omissions.

ISBN 978-1-85524-704-8

Printed by Alfabase, Alphen aan den Rijn, the Netherlands

Contents

INTRODUCTION	1
1 OPERATORS' LICENCES	3
CAR SHARING	3
GROUP HIRE	4
TYPES OF LICENCE	5
2 RUNNING A LOCAL SERVICE	9
QUALITY CONTROL	9
LOCAL SERVICES	10
COMPETITION LAW	14
TENDERED SERVICES	15
CONCESSIONARY FARES	15
COMMUNITY TRANSPORT	16
COMMUNITY BUSES	16
SCHEDULES AND DUTIES	16
CREW ALLOCATION	24
THE DEPOT'S DAILY DUTY ROTA	27
3 DRIVER TRAINING AND DRIVER LICENSING	35
GENERAL INFORMATION	35
PCV DRIVING ENTITLEMENT	41
4 CONDITION OF VEHICLES	51
CONSTRUCTION AND USE REGULATIONS	51
LIGHTING	74
VEHICLE CERTIFICATION, APPROVAL, INSPECTION AND ANNUAL TESTING	79
5 FITNESS, EQUIPMENT AND USE OF PSVs AND MINIBUSES	87
PSV CONDITIONS OF FITNESS	87
EQUIPMENT OF PSVs	99

	USE OF PSVs	100
6	**WORKING TIME FOR DRIVERS, DRIVERS' HOURS AND RECORD KEEPING**	**103**
	WORKING TIME RULES	104
	OFFENCES	108
	"COMMUNITY REGULATED" JOURNEYS	109
	EXEMPTIONS FROM EU RULES	113
	DRIVERS' HOURS OF WORK RECORDS	118
	THE DIGITAL TACHOGRAPH	130
	AETR	133
	BRITISH DOMESTIC OPERATIONS	134
	MIXED DRIVING	136
7	**RESPONSIBILITIES OF THE DRIVER**	**141**
	CUSTOMER CARE — UNDERSTANDING AND HELPING PASSENGERS	141
	CONDUCT OF DRIVERS, PASSENGERS AND OTHERS	145
	ALCOHOL ON COACHES	153
	CLEANLINESS AND FITNESS OF VEHICLES	157
	FARES	157
8	**ACCIDENTS AND INSURANCE**	**165**
	ACCIDENTS	165
	INSURANCE	168
9	**DRIVING OFFENCES**	**171**
	DRINK AND DRIVING	171
	DISQUALIFICATION	173
	OFFENCES FOR WHICH PENALTY POINTS ARE AWARDED	174
	OFFENCES FOR WHICH FINES ARE IMPOSED	175
	REMOVAL OF DISQUALIFICATION	180
	REMOVAL OF ENDORSEMENTS	181
	DUAL LIABILITY	181

10 USE OF VEHICLES ON THE ROAD — 183
- SPEED LIMITS — 183
- LONGER VEHICLES — 185
- USE OF MOBILE TELEPHONES AND/OR MICROPHONES — 185
- DRIVING ON MOTORWAYS — 186
- PEDESTRIAN CROSSINGS AND BUS LANES — 190
- PARKING RESTRICTIONS — 191
- ADVICE ON TAKING A PSV OUTSIDE THE UK — 200

Appendix — 203
- DEFINITIONS — 203
- TERMS — 204

INDEX — 207

INTRODUCTION

It is again my privilege to further update the content of this handbook for the benefit of today's public service vehicle (PSV) drivers.

The demand for previous editions shows that there is an ongoing need for the book which, although of value to all UK PSV drivers, is targeted mainly at the employees of small to medium fleets and owner/operators.

The road passenger transport industry continues to be heavily regulated and the associated legislation places ever-growing demands on both operators and drivers of PSVs. This book gives priority to the requirements of the driver in this respect, especially with regard to the enormous responsibility of carrying passengers safely.

The aim of this book is to assist all coach and bus drivers by putting a comprehensive cross-section of the new and ever-changing rules into plain language. However, the main emphasis is placed upon the knowledge required for legal, safe and efficient operation of PSVs and where the term "driver" is used it refers throughout to the professional drivers of buses and coaches operated for hire and reward under the authority of an operator's licence ("O" licence).

Included in this eighth edition are references to recent legislation on the new EU drivers' hours rules, the associated use of the digital tachograph and the legal requirements for driver training and the qualifications applicable from 2008. In order to keep the information to reasonable proportions, detailed references to Acts of Parliament, etc are omitted. If readers wish to expend their knowledge in this respect, the use of the companion reference book *Croner's Coach and Bus Operations* is recommended.

The UK coach and bus operating industry continues to hold a passenger safety record to be proud of and hopefully this contribution to the professionalism within this field will help to keep this record in place. Drivers who find the handbook of particular interest might wish to consider studying the subject of coach and bus operations in greater depth with a view to enhancing their role and future involvement in this fascinating business which I enjoyed serving for over 40 years.

Brian Hirst

Note: transport law is constantly changing. The contents of this handbook are correct at the time of printing.

August 2007

1 OPERATORS' LICENCES

Before any operator can use a vehicle with nine or more passenger seats to carry passengers for hire or reward he must have a Public Service Vehicle (PSV) operator's licence ("O" licence) granted to him or her by the Traffic Commissioners who are the Government's "Watchdog" for the PSV operating industry.

Hire or reward includes both carriage at separate fares and carriage of a party at a composite fare (private hire).

"Separate fare" covers all payments made by individual passengers, even if not made directly to the driver or operator. For example, an admission ticket for an event which confers a right to be carried on a vehicle to and from the event will be a separate fare and the operator will require a PSV "O" licence.

Where free transport is provided, for example by a firm's "personnel carrier", no "O" licence is needed. But where a business, such as a hotel, uses a passenger carrying vehicle in association with its main activities (in this illustration, as a "courtesy coach") hire or reward exists. (*Rout v Swallow Hotels 1992*) and the operator must have an "O" licence.

Any vehicle with eight or fewer passenger seats which is operated by an "O" licensed operator to carry passengers at separate fares must also be included on the respective PSV "O" licence.

CAR SHARING

The practice of sharing a car or van with eight or fewer seats, for example by employees commuting to the same workplace, is permitted, provided that the fare or fares paid totals less than the running costs of the vehicle, including depreciation.

In such cases, the vehicle is not a PSV, nor is the driver's insurance invalidated by virtue of a "private" vehicle being used "commercially".

GROUP HIRE

Where a party hires a coach, bus or limousine from an operator for a lump sum and then shares the cost amongst its members by charging separate fares, technically even if the vehicle has eight or fewer seats it will be a PSV. In the case of limousines (stretched) with nine or more passenger carrying capacity, these vehicles must be approved by the Vehicle and Operator Services Agency (VOSA) before they can be operated as a PSV

However, operation of privately organised trips at separate fares is widespread and many coach drivers convey such parties on a regular basis. To regularise the practice, the **Public Passenger Vehicles Act 1981** provides that the hire will not be construed as carriage at separate fares if the following conditions are met:

(a) neither the driver, owner nor operator of the vehicle made the arrangements for bringing the party together

(b) the journey has not been previously advertised to the public at large, except by a notice displayed at a place of work, a church or club, or in a journal circulating mainly amongst the relevant employees, worshippers or club members

(c) all passengers make substantially the same journey and there are no fare differences according to time or distance travelled.

Some passenger carrying vehicles need not be operated under a PSV "O" licence. These include Local Education Authorities' school buses (even when also available to the public at large), Community Buses, and buses and minibuses operated non-commercially by social, welfare, religious and educational organisations under a permit.

PSV "O" licences are issued to the operator and do not identify the vehicles which are used under them. The operator receives non-specific licence discs for the number of vehicles in the fleet and these must be displayed on the vehicles.

TYPES OF LICENCE

There are four types of PSV "O" licence issued by Traffic Commissioners:

Standard — national and international	Green discs
Standard national	Blue discs
Restricted	Orange discs
Special restricted	(Orange discs issued to taxi/bus operators)

In addition, Traffic Commissioners can issue Community Bus Permits and permits for "welfare vehicles" (these latter can also be issued by local authorities and other "designated bodies").

A licence will specify the total number of vehicles which can be operated by the licence holder.

Additional vehicles may be temporarily hired in for not more than two weeks and must display the disc of the operator from whom they are hired. In this case that operator (not the hirer) remains the "user" of the vehicle, responsible for its legal and safe operation. Holders of restricted licences cannot hire large buses with more than 16 seats from standard licence holders.

Standard Licences

These permit the operation of any size of PSV. Before the granting of a licence, the operator has to satisfy the Traffic Commissioner that he or she:

(a) has sufficient financial resources to run the vehicles safely — the operator can elect either to maintain them in person or to contract out the maintenance but if it is contracted out, the operator remains responsible for the condition of the vehicles on the road

(b) is of "good repute", ie free of previous convictions relating to the use of a PSV during the last five years; in particular, convictions for a serious offence where a sentence of imprisonment for a term exceeding three months, a fine exceeding level 4 (£2500) on the Standard Scale or a community service order for more than 60 hours was imposed

(c) is professionally competent, or employs a professionally competent transport manager. The operator or the manager must have a PSV CPC national qualification for a Standard "National" licence and a PSV CPC international qualification for a Standard "International" licence.

Traffic Commissioners may suspend, curtail or revoke a PSV "O" licence for breaches of the regulations concerning drivers' hours and records, mechanical condition of the vehicle or contravention of any conditions attached to the licence.

Restricted Licences

An operator may have a restricted licence which covers passenger vehicles with eight or fewer passenger seats, or PSVs with 9–16 seats, exclusive of the driver's seat, which are used non-commercially. Not more than two vehicles per restricted "O" licence may be authorised.

"Non-commercially" in this context is different than in the context of car sharing or permit operation and means any operation which is otherwise than in the course of a business of carrying passengers, or a business conducted by a person whose main occupation is not the operation of PSVs with over eight seats. This would include, for example, the use of a minibus by a taxi firm, whose main business is not PSV operation and whose taxis have eight or fewer seats, or a hotelier whose business is accommodating guests, not carrying passengers. Taxi operators are major users of restricted licences. Another major user is the Post Office (which is not limited to a maximum of two Post Buses!). The holder of a restricted licence does not have to prove professional competence.

Special Restricted Licences

These are issued by Traffic Commissioners to holders of taxi (Hackney Carriage) licences (but not private hire cars), who apply to run a registered local service. There are no requirements as to good repute, financial standing, or professional competence although the holder has to satisfy the local authority's taxi licensing officer that he or she is a fit person to hold a taxi licence and that the vehicle to be used meets prescribed safety standards.

Traffic Commissioners may attach to a special restricted licence a condition that it be used as a PSV only to run a registered local service within the area of the appropriate local licensing authority. When used as a PSV the driver will come within the scope of the domestic drivers' hours regulations but will not need to hold a PCV category D driving licence.

Permits

Permits may be issued by Traffic Commissioners to operators of small buses (9–16 passenger seats) and large buses (over 16 passenger seats). Designated bodies (eg the Scouts Association) may issue them to operators of small buses only.

Permit vehicles, which are used mainly by voluntary organisations such as Community Transport and schools and colleges, may be used to carry passengers for hire and reward provided that:
   (a) the organisation holding the permit operates the vehicles
   (b) they are not available to the public at large
   (c) they are being used non-commercially (ie not for profit)
   (d) they are being used in accordance with any conditions on the permit.

Drivers must either hold a full category D1 driving entitlement or must be a volunteer over the age of 21, have held a full category B entitlement for a minimum of 2 years, and be driving the vehicle for social purposes only.

The maximum authorised mass (laden weight) of the minibus (excluding tail lift if fitted) must not exceed 3.5 tonnes gvw.

A "Permit" disc must be displayed on the vehicle.

Community bus permits

A Community Bus is a vehicle with 9–16 passenger seats operated by a group or groups of persons concerned with the social and welfare needs of a community. Traffic Commissioners can issue Community Bus permits to allow the operators to provide a local service on a non-commercial basis and to carry passengers in other circumstances (eg private hire) to provide revenue to support the Community Bus service.

Currently the driver of a Community Bus must be a volunteer aged 21 years or over and may not receive any payment other than expenses (including loss of earnings). A Community Bus disc must be displayed on the vehicle.

Any local service provided for the public at large by the Community Bus must be registered with the Traffic Commissioners or, in London, provided under a London local service permit issued by Transport for London.

Note: Currently drivers aged 18 years or over who hold a full category D driving entitlement may drive a Community Bus or "Permit" minibus with 9–16 passenger seats (but *not* a large "Permit" bus with 17 or more passenger seats until they reach the age of 21).

2 RUNNING A LOCAL SERVICE

QUALITY CONTROL

Anyone holding a PSV "O" licence may, on giving due notice to the Traffic Commissioners, register and run a local bus service outside London. A service may be withdrawn on giving a similar period of notice. Local Education Authorities running school buses, holders of Community Bus permits and holders of taxi licences who have obtained a Special Restricted PSV "O" licence may also register and operate a local bus service.

Punctuality and Reliability

To aid improvements in the punctuality of local bus services, operators and local authorities are being encouraged by the Department for Transport to form Bus Punctuality Improvement Partnerships. The partnerships must develop a Bus Punctuality Improvement Plan for their respective areas and demonstrate action towards achieving agreed objectives/targets and measurable improvements in the quality and reliability of bus services.

Competition

Thus the operator of a local bus service, even if operating this under a service subsidy agreement for which he or she has successfully tendered, is completely unprotected against competition on the route.

Powers of Traffic Commissioners

Traffic Commissioners require local bus services to be operated in accordance with registered details and to be operated on time. They have powers to stop an operator running a local service and/or impose a financial penalty if the operator fails to run the services on time or at all, or if the operator or an employee can be shown to have "intentionally" interfered in the running of another operator's local service. "On time" has been defined by the Traffic Commissioners as any time within a "six-minute window" of one minute ahead/five minutes behind scheduled arrival/departure time.

Drivers' Behaviour on the Road

It is, therefore, imperative that drivers behave responsibly and do nothing to jeopardise their employer's licence. Competition can only be met legitimately on quality of service, so reliability, timekeeping, good driving and attention to passengers' needs are essential.

LOCAL SERVICES

Local Services (Except London)

A local service is any service on which a passenger can travel a distance of less than 15 miles measured in a straight line.

Local Services (In London)

Within Greater London, a local service can only be operated either by agreement with Transport for London (TFL) (such agreements usually result from successfully tendering for a service) or under a London Service Permit granted by Transport for London.

Timings

Once an operator has registered a local service it must be run strictly in accordance with the registration. Failure to do so, or operation of an unregistered service, can be sufficient reason for a Traffic Commissioner to impose a financial penalty or consider attaching a condition to the "O" licence preventing the operator from running that, or any other, local service.

It is essential that drivers should make use of a reliable watch in order to avoid late operation. *Services should never be operated ahead of schedule.*

Retiming of School Journeys

Sometimes an operator is asked by a school to retime a journey (eg to accommodate an early finish or because of industrial action). This may be done if the service is a dedicated school service paid for by the Local Education Authority but only at the request of the LEA and only for the purpose of enabling the LEA to fulfil its duty to provide free school transport. If the timing of any other service on which school children rely is requested to be altered, the service must still be operated on its registered timing for the benefit of the public at large during the period of notification of the alteration to the Traffic Commissioner.

Duplication

Duplication of a local bus service is permitted but only to provide extra capacity over the whole or part of the route so long as the extra journeys are timed to operate as closely as possible to journeys in the registered timetable.

Traffic Regulation Conditions

Traffic Commissioners sometimes make traffic regulation conditions to reduce the risks of severe traffic congestion or prevent danger to road users or the public in general. These conditions may be attached to an operator's licence and drivers should be aware of them and observe them meticulously. A typical condition may be a ban on picking up or setting down in streets in the immediate vicinity of a bus station, in order to persuade operators to use the bus station and not cause congestion on its approaches. Other examples include controls on vehicle exhaust emissions and noise levels — eg from loudspeaker systems on vehicles.

Bus Stations and Bus Stops

Bus stations are usually operated by Passenger Transport Executive (PTE)s or local authorities, although some remain in private hands. Bus station operators can levy departure charges and allocate stands, although they are legally required to do so as fairly as possible and not to favour any particular operator. Drivers should co-operate with PTE and local authority staff when using bus stations. In particular they should be prepared to move their vehicle from a stand if asked to do so and should avoid interfering with the manoeuvring of competitors' vehicles in the bus station. If their freedom of movement is compromised they should inform both the bus station operator and their employer.

Bus stops are the responsibility of the local highway authority (County Councils, or, in Scotland, Regional Councils) and, in Metropolitan Areas, the PTE. Highway authorities may also make local traffic regulation orders, for example to control picking up and setting down points for excursions and tours, or to limit layover time at city centre kerbside stops.

Hail and Ride

"Hail and Ride" services do not observe bus stops but pick up passengers on being hailed and set them down on request. Drivers on such services must only observe hail and ride working on those sections of the route which the Traffic Commissioner has approved for that purpose. When driving a hail and ride service it is more important than ever to be on the lookout for intending passengers and to show courtesy to other road users by avoiding sudden and unsignalled stops, or stopping at dangerous points such as on the brow of a hill, or in proximity to a road junction or on a bend.

Faretables, Timetables and Destination Notices

Operators must display on a vehicle used on a registered service, or make available on such a vehicle:
- the fare table
- the timetable.

Destination and route number indicators must be displayed correctly and clearly to the exterior of a vehicle used on a registered service.

These conditions do not apply to taxis used on a special restricted "O" licence or to excursions and tours.

Taxis

A taxi (but not a licensed private hire car) may register and run a local service if the operator has obtained a special restricted operator's licence.

In addition, taxis may be hired at separate fares from authorised places, ie specially designated ranks, at which taxis to common destinations may ply for hire. They must display a "Shared Taxi" sign, and *may not* ply for hire at separate fares by cruising along a bus route but the driver may "tout" for business at the designated ranks. He must do so in an orderly way, by word of mouth only, and within 6m of his taxi.

Taxis and private hire cars may also be pre-booked at separate fares.

Drivers of PSVs should not interfere with taxi operators but may report any transgressors of the above rules to the local taxi licensing officer, or, in the case of the operator of a taxi or bus running a local service, to the Traffic Commissioner.

Fuel Tax Rebates

Operators of local services, and of some scheduled express services, receive rebates of fuel tax under a scheme currently known as the Bus Service Operators' Grant (BSOG). If the Traffic Commissioner finds that any operator has intentionally interfered in the operation of another operator's local service, or failed to operate a local service as registered, or run an unregistered local service, then the Commissioner has powers under the **Transport Act 1985** and **Transport Act 2000** (as amended) to apply one or both of the following penalties:
  (a) the prohibition of the operation of a specified or any local service
  (b) the payment of sums up to £550 per vehicle used under the operator's "O" licence.

COMPETITION LAW

Competition law applies to the bus industry in exactly the same way as it applies to traders in the High Street.

Any agreement made between two or more operators in which they voluntarily accept restrictions on their ability to compete is registerable with, and comes under the scrutiny of, the Office of Fair Trading (OFT). This will include any agreements on joint operations, tendering, ticketing or route sharing. The OFT may of course decide that the agreement is not potentially harmful to the public or designed to exclude a competitor and permit it.

Unfair competitive practices, especially the practice known as "predatory pricing" where a large operator drops bus fares to an uneconomic level to drive a competitor off "his" route can also be investigated by the OFT.

Drivers should be on the look out for restrictive and anti-competitive practices and report these to their employers, or complain to the OFT.

TENDERED SERVICES

Schools contracts are often seen as an operator's bread and butter income. These, together with any socially desirable services which no operator has registered because takings are too low, are put out to tender by County and Regional (in Scotland) Councils and PTEs (in Metropolitan Areas).

Drivers operating tendered services should be especially vigilant to ensure that no journeys are lost and must report any lost mileage immediately. Failure to do so can result in loss of the service subsidy contract.

In addition, some tenders are won on the basis of quoting for a service operating cost with the tendering authority retaining the income from passenger fares (revenue). In such instances drivers must be able to account fully for all revenue, especially if their vehicle is boarded by a tendering authority's inspector.

CONCESSIONARY FARES

County, District and Regional Councils and, in Metropolitan Areas, PTEs, have powers to make concessionary fares schemes for: pensioners; children under 17; scholars age 17–19; blind and disabled persons. These may take the form of free travel, tokens, or permits allowing reduced fares either all day or at off peak times.

The above authorities also have powers to serve compulsory participation notices upon operators providing local services in their area.

Drivers should familiarise themselves with their local concessionary fares schemes and co-operate in operating them. In particular they must permit inspectors and data collectors employed by the above authorities to board their buses to make fare checks and collect data.

COMMUNITY TRANSPORT

Vehicles operated by Community Transport organisations do carry passengers at separate fares. However, drivers should be aware that services such as Disabled Dial a Ride are not in competition since:
  (a) they are not available to the public at large
  (b) they are operated under the minibus permit regulations and
  (c) they are frequently subsidised by the local authority or PTE.

Community Transport operations are allowed by virtue of operator's "Section 19" Permits (**Transport Act 1985**).

COMMUNITY BUSES

Community Bus services are provided by organisations using volunteer drivers operating 9–16 passenger seat minibuses. They are registered local services running to a published timetable and available to the general public in the same way as a local service operated under an "O" licence..

"Community Bus" operators are authorised by virtue of an operator's "Section 22" Permit (see *Permits*).

SCHEDULES AND DUTIES

Driving on a public passenger transport service is not a "nine-to-five" job and inevitably involves working unsocial hours.

In the case of some local urban and inter-urban services the first vehicle often leaves the depot before dawn and the last vehicle arrives back at the depot close to midnight. In express service operation, nights out for both vehicles and crews are not uncommon.

Scheduling a fleet of vehicles and allocating staff to them so as to provide the best service in the most economical manner is an art. The scheduler produces an interdependent set of timetables, individual vehicle timings, a duty roster and a rota of individuals' daily duties.

Drivers do not need to be able to prepare these documents but it is essential that they can read and understand them. The smooth working of the undertaking relies on staff reporting for duty punctually, relieving earlier drivers or crews at the right time and following the instructions on the vehicle running board regarding the operation of the service(s).

Schedules not only affect drivers' working lives but their social and domestic lives as well. Workable schedules and rotas which staff perceive to be "fair" improve drivers' working conditions and help retain a satisfied and well motivated workforce. This, in turn, leads to a better and more reliable service to the public and enhances employees' job security.

The Service Timetable

Many operators issue their drivers with copies of the service timetables which they also make available to the public. In any case, one of the conditions attached to registration of a local service is that the timetable and faretable are carried or displayed on the vehicle.

Often the vehicle running board will only show timings at route termini and perhaps one or two main points en route and the service timetable is then the only means the driver has of knowing his expected time at intermediate points.

Delays to services are often inescapable but running ahead of time is inexcusable. Apart from possible disciplinary action against the driver, early running can result in loss of revenue through missed passengers, loss of passenger goodwill, or the danger that the undertaking may be reported to the Traffic Commissioners for failing to provide a service as registered, which could lead to sanctions against the operator's licence.

Drivers who are detailed to run a duplicate service should also be aware of, and try to comply with, the rules which Traffic Commissioners are applying to such services. These are that duplication should only take place to provide extra journeys over the whole or part of the route and that these journeys should be timed to run as closely as possible to the registered timetable.

Failure to comply with these simple rules could, wherever there is a competing service on the route, be construed as interference in the operation of another registered service.

The service timetable may employ either the 24 hour clock or am/pm timings.

Conventionally the timing points on the route are listed down a column at the left hand side of the page and the timings for each journey are given in further columns to the right of this. Separate tables are prepared for journeys in either direction and sometimes for Saturdays, Sundays and Bank Holidays, or summer and winter services.

Example of Typical Timetable for a Local Bus Service

STALYBRIDGE—OLDHAM

Mondays to Saturdays

	NS	NS				NS			
STALYBRIDGE, Bus Station	0715	0745	0845		1645	1715	1945		2245
Stamford Park	0718	0748	0848	AND	1648	1718	1948	AND	2248
Hurst Cross	0722	0752	0852	EVERY	1652	1722	1952	EVERY	2252
Abbeyhills, Welcome Inn	0730	0800	0900	HOUR	1700	1730	1956	HOUR	2258
OLDHAM, Town Square	0738	0808	0908	UNTIL	1708	1738	2006	UNTIL	2306

Sundays

STALYBRIDGE, Bus Station	1345		2245
Stamford Park	1348	AND	2248
Hurst Cross	1352	EVERY	2252
Abbeyhills, Welcome Inn	1358	HOUR	2258
OLDHAM, Town Square	1408	UNTIL	2306

NS - Not Saturdays

Codes at the head of each column give additional information. Standard abbreviations are M, T, W, Th, F, S, Su for the days of the week, plus the letters X for Excepted and O for Only, thus:

MO = Mondays only
SSuX = Saturdays and Sundays excepted.

Other letters and symbols are used to indicate journeys which operate:

Schooldays only
Market days only
Bank Holidays only or excepted summer Sundays, etc.

Codes beside timings may indicate picking up and setting down restrictions, and timing information such as:
u — stops to pick up only
s — stops to set down only

a — arrival time
d — departure time

A few undertakings issue non-conventional timetables with, for example, timings and timing points shown in rows rather than columns (see below), or with lists of departure times from main points with running times in minutes to intermediate points. Whilst these are brief and less bulky than conventional timetables they are also more difficult to use for both drivers and passengers.

Example of Timetable in Columnar Form

BUS STN	RAIL STN	NEAR TOWN	FAR TOWN
0900	0905	0915	0928
1000	1005	1015	1028
1100	1105	1115	1128
1200	1205	1215	1228
1300	1305	1315	1328

The Bus Running Board

While the service timetable shows all the journeys made by all the vehicles on the route, the running boards which are prepared for each vehicle show only the specific journeys to be operated by that vehicle.

Since some service buses may be on the road for as long as 18 hours and may make journeys on more than one service, the same running board may be used in the course of a day by more than one driver. As it relates primarily to the work done by the bus and only incidentally to some or all of the driver's duties it should be left on the vehicle.

Running boards often contain a mass of information not shown on the service timetable, for example descriptions of turning manoeuvres to be performed at termini, instructions to run "dead" or out of service between certain trips, or between depot and termini, or details of timed connections to be made (eg at a rail station).

Example of Running Board

Days of Operation	Leave Depot
WEEKDAYS	0630

Running Board No.
1

Service No.	1	1	2	2	1	1	2	2	1	1	2	2	1	1	2	2	1	1
BUS STATION	0625	0725	0730	0830	0835	0925	0930	1030	1035	1125	1130	1230	1235	1325	1330	1430	1435	1525
MOOR HILL	0658	0703	↓	↑	0858	0903	↓	↑	1058	1103	↓	↑	1258	1303	↓	↑	1458	1503
MILL GATE			0743	0818			0943	1018			1143	1218			1343	1418		
LITTLEFOLD			0758	0801			0958	1003			1158	1203			1358	1403		

Service No.	2	2	1	1	2	2	1	1	2	2	1	1	2	2	1	1		
BUS STATION	1530	1630	1635	1725	1730	1830	1835	1925	1930	2030	2035	2125	2130	2230	2235	2315	2330	
MOOR HILL	↓	↑	1658	1703	↓	↑	1858	1903	↓	↑	2058	2103	↓	↑	2258	2303		
MILL GATE	1543	1618			1743	1818			1943	2018			2143	2218				
LITTLEFOLD	1550	1603			1758	1803			1958	2003			2158	2203				
																		↓
DEPOT																		2335

From	To	Duty	
0630	1035	4	
1035	1330	3	
1330	1835	33	
1835	2335	11	

There are many different running board formats. Nowadays these are often computer print-outs. Usually, like the service timetable, they have timing points in the left hand column, and timings of each trip in columns to the right of this. There the similarities end. Timings in both directions are usually shown, reading both up and down columns. Arrows are frequently used to indicate the direction of travel of the vehicle.

Some running boards have timing points at the head of each column and times in rows below these. A few operators produce running boards which could more accurately be described as "duty boards" since they contain details of all the trips to be performed by a driver working a specific period on duty. This type of board can be removed from one vehicle and taken to the next vehicle to be driven (perhaps after a meal break) since they are essentially a consolidation of extracts from the running boards of all the vehicles to be driven while working that duty.

There are a number of points which drivers can bear in mind when studying their running boards.

1. *Interworking* — a vehicle may be switched from one route to another in order to maximise its productivity. For example, a works journey to an industrial estate may be linked with a following school journey from an adjacent housing estate.

    A more usual reason for switching vehicles between routes is to reduce the total number of vehicles required. Where two or more routes meet at a common point, such as a bus station, and the total of all the "layovers" or standing times of all the vehicles on the routes would be sufficient to perform a complete round trip, the vehicles may be rescheduled to interwork between the routes and thereby save a vehicle. It is important of course that a minimum agreed layover time still remains for each vehicle at its trip end.

2. *Tidal flow operation* — at peak times when the majority of passengers are travelling in one direction, eg into town in the morning peak, it makes sense to maximise the number of vehicles in service in that direction. Some vehicles can be scheduled to run empty back to outer termini "out of service" so as to be available there more quickly and perform an additional inward journey which will still be in

the peak hour. For the sake of good passenger relations it is essential that the vehicle destination blinds on light trips clearly indicate that the vehicle is not in service.

3. *Drop back vehicles* — a vehicle may be brought out of depot to perform one round trip on a service and this journey may be included in part of a driver's duty. Although this is often done simply to duplicate journeys at times of peak demand, two other reasons for slotting a "drop back" into a service are:

   (a) to enable a service affected by congestion to recover to its schedule timetable — the extra bus is slotted into the service at the start of the morning or evening peak and all buses on the route "drop back" to the timing of the following vehicle; by the time the extra bus has performed a round trip it will arrive back at the point where it was slotted in simultaneously with a service bus and one or other of the vehicles can be returned to depot

   (b) to cover meal breaks — the extra bus takes over the journey which the driver taking the meal break would have operated; all buses on the service then drop back as described above, enabling their drivers to take a meal break equivalent to the headway between vehicles (the drop back bus or buses can be returned to depot when all meal breaks have been completed).

For example — if the round trip running time (including five minutes layover at each end of the route) on a service run with four vehicles is 60 minutes, departures from the bus station could be at:

Bus No. 1	00 minutes past the hour
Bus No. 2	15 minutes past the hour
Bus No. 3	30 minutes past the hour
Bus No. 4	45 minutes past the hour
Bus No. 1	00 minutes past the next hour

Inserting an extra bus on the hour allows bus No. 1 to take over the 15 minutes past departure, No. 2 the 30 minutes past, etc. On the next hour, Bus No. 4 and the extra bus will arrive simultaneously at the bus station, and the extra bus or Bus No. 4 can be returned to depot without destroying the basic 15 minute headway on the service.

4. *Frequency changes* — lower frequencies are usually provided between peak periods, in the evenings and on Sundays. At the times when frequencies are changed the driver may notice that the pattern of departure times from termini alters. For example, with departures on the hour and every 20 minutes a change from three to two buses per hour will change the departures at 20 and 40 minutes past the hour to one at half past the hour.

5. *Differential running times* — whilst it is often difficult to run to time in the peak hours, it is also often frustrating for both drivers and passengers if time has to be spent in the off peak waiting at timing points to avoid running early. For this reason the running times allowed on a route are sometimes adjusted at different times of the day to take account of traffic congestion and heavier passenger loadings.

CREW ALLOCATION

The United Kingdom ("Domestic") and EU drivers' hours regulations and Working Time Regulations set an upper limit on the amount of work which can be allocated daily and weekly to drivers.

Daily Limits

The maximum length of time for which a driver on "Domestic" rules journeys and work (which includes most regular local services) can drive without taking a break of at least 30 minutes is 5½ hours. This may be extended to 8½ hours if the combined total of all the breaks in that period is not less than 45 minutes. The driver must in addition have a break of at least 30 minutes at the end of this period unless it is the end of the working day. The maximum total driving time is 10 hours. The working day must not exceed 16 hours and the driver must normally have 10 hours' rest between working days; this may be reduced to 8½ hours on three occasions each week.

On duties regulated by the EU drivers' hours (mainly express and private hire work) the maximum aggregate driving time without a break (or breaks) of at least (or amounting to) 45 minutes is 4½ hours. The maximum total daily driving time is normally nine hours but can be 10 hours twice in a fixed week. The driver must have 11 hours' rest in every 24 hours; this may be reduced to nine hours on three occasions between weekly rest periods. The minimum daily rest if the vehicle is double manned is nine hours in every 30 hours.

The EU drivers' hours rules changed in April 2007 (see *Working Time*).

Weekly Limits

"Domestic" hours drivers must have a fortnightly rest of 24 hours, and EU hours drivers must have a weekly rest of 45 hours after six consecutive days' driving, although there are relaxations of this rule.

All drivers are entitled under the Working Time Regulations to limit their maximum average weekly working hours to 48. "Domestic" hours drivers can "opt out" of this limit by agreement with their employers but drivers who work under the EU hours rules cannot opt out.

The above is a necessarily brief resumé of the drivers' hours limits which affect the allocation of drivers and crews to vehicles. Full details are given under *Working Time and Drivers' Hours*.

In addition to statutory limits on hours of work, many drivers are covered by trade union agreements which also affect their duties. These generally cover matters outside the statutory limits, such as the maximum number of "split" duties to be included within a roster and travelling times between relief points and the place where meal breaks are taken.

Driving Duties

Duties are usually arranged in such a way that a driver is allocated to a vehicle in service for a portion of its time on the road before being relieved for a meal break. After his meal break the driver is then allocated to another vehicle for the remainder of his time "on duty" or "shift".

Overtime

In making up duties or "shifts", schedulers sometimes leave small portions of work unallocated, to be staffed on an overtime basis.

Allocators and drivers have a duty to ensure that in detailing a driver to, or volunteering for, such an overtime portion, none of the following are exceeded or encroached upon:
- maximum daily driving time
- daily spreadover limits
- minimum daily rest periods
- minimum weekly or fortnightly rest periods
- maximum average weekly "working time" limit
- "reference period" limits
- limits on "mixed" "domestic" or EU hours, driving where these apply (see *Drivers' Hours*).

Some undertakings have negotiated standard weekly payments for drivers which equate with an average week's work on a roster containing some scheduled overtime. The rosters are arranged to even out the work done over a fixed period. Rest day working (see below) is usually still voluntary and not included in this averaging.

Types of Duty

To cover all the services in a full working day some staff will have to start work early and could be coming off duty even before midday, others will have to start late and work through to nearly midnight and yet others will be needed to cover the work in the middle of the day. In addition, because there will be extra vehicles out in the morning and evening peaks, some staff will need to perform split duties, with a period off duty between their two periods of work. A roster or "rota" (see below) is drawn up and posted well in advance to spread this work on a rotating basis and to acquaint staff with their personal duty patterns for the coming months.

Trade union agreements usually define different types of duties in some way so that allocators and staff know the time boundaries within which they are working. A typical agreement would be:

Early duty:	Finishing no later than 15.30
Middle duty:	Finishing no later than 20.00
Late duty:	Finishing after 20.00
Split duty:	Covering two work portions (usually in the morning and evening peak periods) and with an intermediate off duty period. This may be "paid through" and be of some duration between maximum and minimum limits, eg over 1½ but less than four hours.

THE DEPOT'S DAILY DUTY ROTA

Size of the Rota

An estimate of the number of duties which will have to be worked by the staff at a depot in order to drive all the vehicles in service can be made by dividing the total number of bus hours by the average work content (ie ignoring signing on and off times, meal breaks and any time spent by a driver travelling on foot or as a passenger to take over a bus).

Linking portions of work together in the most economic way so as to get the most productivity from bus drivers or crews is an art; the result being the list of numbered duties which are posted in the depot; usually in strict order of their starting times.

A typical duty line on a rota may look like this.

Extract from Duty Rota

Duty No.	Sign On	Take over		Bus No.	Relieved		Sign Off	Hours	Pay
		Time	Place		Time	Place			
M.1	1210	1230	Bus Stn	3	1615	Bus Stn			
		1645	Bus Stn	2	1940	Bus Stn			
		1945	Stand 1	4	1950	Garage	2000	7.50	8.00

Note: M.1 — this is classed as a middle duty.

Sign on 12.10 — as well as a signing on time allowance to enable the driver to collect a ticket machine, make up a waybill, etc to find, check and take over the bus allocated to running board 3 and if necessary set the destination blinds, there may be an additional travelling allowance to enable the driver to reach the take-over point if this is, as in this case, not the depot where he or she signs on.

16.15 to 16.45 — meal break and statutory break. Take over Bus 2 at 16.45 in the bus station.

19.40 to 19.45 — take over Bus 4. The five minutes allowed may include a couple of minutes travelling time to an adjacent stand, perhaps in the street outside the bus station.

19.50 — both the bus and the driver return to depot. 10 minutes signing off allowance given.

7.50 — time from signing on to signing off.

8.00 — time value of the duty for payment purposes. In this case it probably represents a negotiated minimum day's pay.

Note: The meal break is also "paid through" in this case. In some organisations, "paid through" spreadover duties have been negotiated. In others, payment may be at time and a half because of factors like Sunday working, extra late finishing, etc.

Standby duties are also written into the rota so that the signing on and off times can be known in advance. Usually these correspond roughly to the type of duty which the relief replaces in the roster pattern. Occasionally there are portions of duties which contain no work content (eg the second half of a late duty) and these may be marked on the rota with an instruction such as "Enquire" which indicates that the driver can be asked to stand by for that time period.

Sometimes if the depot is fully staffed and there are no obvious problems the allocator or inspector may allow the driver to sign off without incurring any pay penalties.

It may even be in the interests of an allocator to sign a driver off early in order to bring him in early the next day without infringing his statutory daily rest allowance.

Drivers should note in this case that although they may be rostered and paid for working until late, so far as their statutory hours are concerned, what counts is the time they are actually on duty, not the time they are rostered.

Duty Rosters

In the duty roster which accompanies the rota staff are allocated a numbered duty for every day on which they are scheduled to work. Some rosters are for seven days with an allocated rest day (and the opportunity to work overtime on one rest day per fortnight on domestic work). Others are for five days with certain rest days "starred" to indicate an overtime opportunity. (These are more common where the bulk of weekend work is performed by part time staff.)

To comply with drivers' hours regulations and union agreements rosters are usually drawn up so that a long weekend is scheduled each month and no late duty is followed by an early duty.

Some duties are "stand by" duties to cover for sickness and absenteeism, others are "regular reliefs" to cover specific types of duty left uncovered by a driver or crew being scheduled for a rest day.

Roster length

The total number of daily duties in a week (ie five times the number of duties on the daily rota plus the Saturday and Sunday rota) divided by the length of the working week gives an indication of the size of the roster. For example, if there are 61 duties in a week and staff work five days, this will give a roster length of 13 weeks with four "spare" or standby duties.

The length of a roster can be reduced by splitting it — for example by allocating a group of drivers to a restricted number of routes.

The number of split duties will also depend upon the severity of the peak hour demands in relation to the off peak traffic, in particular the extent to which operating frequencies have to be increased in the peak, or additional traffic can be generated in the off peak to avoid operating too many part time vehicles.

Duty Postings

Name	Week numbers for weeks commencing:				
	May 4	May 11	May 18	May 25	etc
Smith	1	2	3	4	5
Jones	2	3	4	5	6
Williams	3	4	5	6	7
Green	4	5	6	7	8
etc...					

Finding your way around the duty rota and roster
Drivers normally work their way through the roster to which they are allocated. Thus if in the current week a driver is on week 1 of the roster given as an example below, he or she will work late duties M-F and have S and Su off.

The following week he or she will work week 2, having M and Tu off (providing the monthly long weekend) and then commence early duties. Note that for the purposes of drivers' hours this prevents an early duty following a late duty the previous night.

The rota will contain details of the work content of all the duties, so that a driver allocated to M.1 on M and Tu of Week 4 will be able to ascertain that on those days he or she will sign on at 12.10 and sign off at 20.00.

A typical short (12 week) duty roster may look like the example given below. It should be emphasised that this is only an example and is not a model of all rosters.

Each individual undertaking will have its own negotiated roster pattern which will contain only some of the features of this example.

Duty schedules and rosters are complicated (see example below). They are also sometimes changed at short notice to accommodate traffic irregularities.

3 DRIVER TRAINING AND DRIVER LICENSING

GENERAL INFORMATION

Driver Certificate of Professional Competence

Currently the only practical qualification required by a person seeking to become a driver of Public Service Vehicles (PSVs) is the holding of the relevant (Category D or D1) Passenger Carrying Vehicle (PCV) driving licence. This changes on 10 September 2008, when the EU Vocational Training Directive comes into effect.

The directive requires a PCV licence holder seeking to become a PSV driver to obtain a Certificate of Professional Competence (CPC) in PSV driving. The PCV licence holder will be able to undergo the relevant training and examinations whilst being employed by a PSV operator but non-licence holders will have to undergo the training before taking the tests to obtain the relevant PCV licence.

The training requirements for the CPC are broader than that currently required to obtain a PCV driving licence and are aimed at improving road and passenger safety, passenger comfort, reducing fuel consumption and reducing environmental damage. The training will be undergone both initially (when acquiring the driving licence) and periodically thereafter. From September 2008, all non-PCV licence holders seeking to become PSV drivers will be required to undertake four hours of theory tests and a two-hour practical test to obtain both the relevant PCV driving licence and the Driver's CPC qualification. All existing PSV drivers will have to undergo and complete periodic training of at least 35 hours by September 2013 in sessions of at least seven hours in order to obtain and retain their (CPC) qualification and their existing PCV licence.

The training, in addition to driving tuition, will cover drivers' hours, tachographs, working time, seat belt law, safety equipment, vehicle loading and luggage handling, health and safety and risk awareness, effects of fatigue, stress, alcohol and drugs, healthy eating, travel documentation, action in emergencies and first aid, vehicle evacuation techniques, accident reports, standards of service, customer relations, role of the driver in the company and customer service, vehicle maintenance, company organisation, the economic environment of the carriage of passengers and the organisation of the market.

The cost of the tests for new licence applicants will increase due to the longer tests involved. The Theory Test will cost £75 and the Practical Driving Test will cost £130.

Driver Licensing (Third EU Directive on Driving Licences)

The current regulations on driving entitlements are shown below, however new regulations implementing the requirements of the Third EU Directive on Driving Licences will be progressively introduced from 2008 to 2013. The various different types (110) of driving licences existing within the recently expanded European Community will be gradually reduced to a common single model licence in plastic card format — similar to the current UK photocard licence but without the paper counterpart. A microchip in the card will carry the minimum information specified at the time by the European Commission.

The definitions of vehicle categories for driving entitlement purposes will be aligned to EU vehicle type approval legislation and new licences will recognise the new definitions. However, existing drivers will retain their existing entitlements under "grandfather rights". New minimum requirements for the driving test for each entitlement category will be introduced along with revised medical standards and driver training requirements (see *EU Driver Training Directive* above).

Revised minimum age limits will be introduced for new licence applicants and the maximum validity of a new vocational, eg PSV, driving licence will be five years, and renewal will be subject to the driver concerned meeting the CPC qualification and the required medical standards on each renewal occasion.

Qualifying for a Licence

Currently a driving licence may be obtained if, during the past two years the applicant has:
   (a) held a full licence
   (b) passed a driving test
   (c) held a full licence issued in Northern Ireland, the Isle of Man or the Channel Islands.

Classes of Licence (Current)

1. Provisional licence.
2. Ordinary driving entitlement (category B).
3. Passenger Carrying Vehicle (PCV) driving entitlement (category D).
4. Large Goods Vehicle (LGV) driving entitlement (category C).
5. Visitor's driving licence.

A provisional licence for the relevant driving authority must be obtained in order to take a vehicle on the road for the purpose of learning to drive and taking the regulation test.

The holder of a provisional licence may drive vehicles of a class authorised on that licence only when accompanied by, and under the supervision of, a qualified driver who must be at least 21 years of age and have held a relevant full licence or a combination of relevant licences for at least three years. The vehicle must display "L" plates.

Application forms for most types of provisional licence are obtainable from post offices and when completed should be sent to the Driver and Vehicle Licensing Centre (DVLC) Swansea together with the appropriate fee (see *Cost and duration of licences*). However, this does not apply for a provisional PCV (category D) licence which is dealt with as a separate item in this section

There are different categories of vehicles for driving licence purposes (classified A–P) each entitling a driver to drive the vehicles in that class.

A test passed on a vehicle with automatic transmission restricts driving to that type of vehicle in that driving licence class. A further test must be taken before driving a vehicle in that class with manual transmission.

Provisional licence holders must pass a written theory test before taking the practical test for a full category B entitlement to drive motor vehicles up to 3.5 tonnes gvw and with less than nine passenger seats.

Once these tests have been passed and a full category B entitlement has been gained, the driver can then apply for a provisional licence to drive vehicles either in category D (passenger carrying vehicles with more than eight passenger seats) or D1 (passenger carrying vehicles with between 9 and 16 passenger seats), or C or C1 (large goods vehicles).

An application for a provisional licence must be made which also entails submitting a medical report. On passing a D/D1 test, including a theory test (which must be passed first) the driver is then allowed to drive large/small passenger vehicles respectively for hire or reward or otherwise (see *PCV Driving Test*).

New drivers holding only a category B entitlement may drive vehicles in category D1 on behalf of a non-commercial body under the following conditions:
- a full licence has been held for at least two years
- the driver is aged 21 years or over
- no payment or any other consideration is received other than out of pocket expenses

- the vehicle is being driven for social purposes only
- there is no trailer attached to the vehicle
- the maximum authorised mass of the vehicle does not exceed 3.5 tonnes (excluding specialised equipment used for disabled passengers)
- does not exceed 4.25 tonnes in other circumstances.

It is an offence to drive a vehicle on a public road unless the driver holds the appropriate licence for that particular class of vehicle.

The cost of a theoretical test is £21.50 and the standard driving test currently costs £89.00 (Monday/Friday up to 16.30 hours). For tests conducted after this time and on Saturdays the cost is £107.00.

Towing trailers

Drivers wishing to tow heavy trailers (those weighing more than 750kg maximum authorised mass (MAM)) must hold a full licence for the type of rigid vehicle (tractor unit) concerned, before taking the practical driving test for the trailer licence category D + E or D1 + E licence.

Minimum age limits

No person under the age of 16 is allowed to drive a motor vehicle on the roads. The current minimum ages for driving the various groups of passenger vehicles are:

Small passenger vehicle, ie constructed or adapted to carry not more than eight persons excluding the driver, or *small goods vehicle*, ie constructed or adapted to carry or to haul goods and not adapted to carry more than eight persons excluding the driver and not exceeding 3.5t permissible maximum weight (including the weight of any trailer drawn not exceeding 750kg gross)

17 years or 16 years if a disabled person receiving a mobility allowance under s.37A of the **Social Security Act 1975**

Large passenger vehicle, ie constructed or adapted to carry more than eight persons excluding the driver	21* years
Large goods vehicles exceeding 7.5 tonnes permissible maximum weight (including the weight of any trailer drawn), articulated vehicles.	21 years

*but see *Minimum ages of drivers*

The age limits shown do not apply to vehicles owned or driven under orders of HM Forces.

Cost and Duration of Licences

Car provisional licence (valid until the holder's 70th birthday) with conversion to full licence after passing driving test	£45
Exchange licence when additional group of vehicles added	free
Passenger Carrying Vehicle Provisional Licence	free
Full Passenger Carrying Vehicle (PCV) entitlement in exchange for Provisional	free

Renewal and Replacement

A driving licence must be renewed on or before the date of expiry. No days of grace are allowed. This is currently free of charge. Licences lost of defaced may be replaced at a cost of £22.

Note: These fees are subject to change.

Production of Licence

A police officer can demand the production of a driving licence for examination and if it is not immediately available it is a defence to show that the driver:

(a) produced it at a police station of his or her choice within seven days, or

(b) produced it there as soon as possible, or
(c) due to circumstances it was not reasonably practicable to produce the licence before the day on which proceedings for not producing the licence were commenced.

Remember that a driver must have a current ordinary licence with PCV entitlement (where applicable), and this must be signed. This is a legal requirement.

PCV DRIVING ENTITLEMENT

On 1 April 1991 the United Kingdom fully implemented the provisions in the **Road Traffic (Driver Licences and Information Systems) Act 1989** and the **Motor Vehicles (Driving Licences) (Large Goods Vehicles and Passenger Carrying Vehicles) Regulations 1990** which provided for a unified driver licensing system conforming to the requirements of EC Directive 80/1263. Further legislation was necessary to introduce the requirements of the Second EC Directive on Driving Licences, which introduced the concept of indefinite mutual recognition of licences in all EU Member States, together with common standards of health and competence. The current regulations governing driving entitlements are contained in the **Driving Licences (Community Driving Licence) Regulations 1996** and the **Motor Vehicles (Driving Licences) Regulations 1999** (SI 1995 No. 2864 — as amended).

The regulations which bring the United Kingdom into line with European Community practice provide that:

(a) the previous separation of driving licences into vocational licences (issued by Traffic Commissioners from Traffic Area Offices) and ordinary driving licences issued by the DVLC at Swansea ceased subject to there being transitional arrangements covering the currency of existing vocational licences

(b) there is now a unified licence showing driving entitlement for all vehicles issued centrally by DVLC, henceforth the licensing authority for the issue of all driving licences. However, Traffic Commissioners retain their disciplinary powers in relation to drivers of Public Service Vehicles (PSVs), ie "O" licensed (Hire or Reward) vehicles

(c) higher medical standards are required for Passenger Carrying Vehicle (PCV) drivers — epileptics, diabetics receiving insulin treatment and drivers falling below new eyesight standards (including monocular drivers) will not be issued with PCV licences (existing drivers who obtained their vocational entitlement before 1 January 1997 and who can show regular PCV driving before then and who have not been involved in an eyesight related accident in the previous 10 years may not be required to meet the standard applying now

(d) there are also some relaxations from (c) other than for certain epileptics who may not receive PCV entitlement.

   Note: *Epileptics may apply for PCV entitlement subject to being able to satisfy certain conditions.*

(e) medical reports are required on applying for a PCV entitlement or renewing a PCV entitlement from age 45 onwards. PCV entitlement is valid until age 45; thereafter renewals must be made every five years and annually from the age of 65. There is an obligation for licence holders to notify DVLC if an illness or disability is expected to last more than three months, or worsens, if this is likely to affect their driving.

Categories of PCV Entitlement

Category D — large passenger carrying vehicle with nine or more passenger seats (including articulated buses).
Category D+E — buses towing trailers over 750kg gvw.
Category D1 — PCVs (minibuses 9–16 passenger seats).

Passenger Carrying Vehicles (PCVs)

The driving licence regulations no longer distinguish between PSVs and non PSVs. All buses, whether or not used for hire and reward, are classed as PCVs. Thus a category D or D1 entitlement is required to drive a PCV not used for hire and reward, but a PSV with eight or fewer passenger seats can now be driven on a Category B entitlement (which covers motor vehicles with eight or fewer passenger seats not exceeding 3.5t gvw). Drivers of school buses owned by Local Education Authorities (LEAs) require category D entitlement, but not drivers of Community or "Permit" minibuses.

PCV Driving Test

Drivers must hold a full category B entitlement before applying for a licence showing *provisional* category D, or D1, (PCV) entitlement. This requirement, called staging, effectively prevents the conduct of dual ordinary/vocational driving tests.

The application must be made to the DVLA and can be made up to three months in advance of the licence being required, accompanied by a medical report which must be signed by a doctor not more than four months prior to the date the licence is to take effect. A fee for the provisional licence will be payable (see *Cost and Duration of Licences*).

Application for a PCV driving test is made to the Driving Standards Agency and should be accompanied by the appropriate test fee. The test comprises a theory test and a practical test.

The test may be conducted by:
(a) a PCV examiner employed by the Driving Standards Agency
(b) an examiner employed by a PSV operator and approved by the DfT to carry out tests on behalf of that operator
(c) persons authorised by the armed forces, a fire brigade or police authority for employees engaged in driving their vehicles.

The examiner will test the applicant's competence and in particular will have regard to the following items:
- knowledge of the highway code
- competence to drive the vehicle and, if necessary, couple and de-couple the trailer.
- knowledge of components relating to the safety of the vehicle
- ability to demonstrate describe or perform random technical checks on their test vehicle, relating to:
  - fluid levels
  - tyres and wheels
  - steering
  - brakes
  - lighting
  - audible warnings
  - instruments
  - air tanks
  - loading

The PCV driving test is currently similar in most respects to the LGV driving test in that both are of the same duration (1½ hours) and are conducted partly on the public road and partly off it (to test manoeuvring skills).

On passing the test a driver will have a full PCV driving entitlement once DVLC receives:
(a) the test pass certificate
(b) the provisional category D licence (for addition of full entitlement).

Minimum Test Vehicles

From 1 January 2007 a minimum test vehicle for a category D driving test must be fitted with a working tachograph and anti-lock brakes (ABS), must be at least 10 metres long and at least 2.4 metres wide and capable of attaining a speed of 80kph on the level.

The same minimum test vehicle may be used for a category D + E driving test providing it is drawing a closed box trailer of at least 1250kg gvw and is at least 2.4 metres wide and 2 metres high.

A driver with provisional category D entitlement who passes a PCV driving test in a vehicle with 9–16 passenger seats will obtain a *category D1 (9–16 passenger seats)* PCV entitlement which will only entitle the driver to drive a passenger vehicle with no more than 16 passenger seats for hire and reward. Minimum test vehicles for category DI tests must weight at least 4 tonnes and be at least 5 metres in length. The speed and braking requirements are as for category D minimum test vehicles.

Preparation for the Tests

Applicants should study:
- (a) the Highway Code
- (b) DfT Pamphlet — *Your Driving Test*
- (c) *Driving* — The DfT manual from HMSO and most bookshops
- (d) "The Theory Test for Large Vehicle Drivers" — from The Stationery Office.

They should also make sure they know the rules regarding:
- (a) equipment which must by law be carried on a PSV
- (b) conduct of drivers and passengers
- (c) drivers' hours and records regulations
- (d) drivers' responsibilities after an accident.

Applicants should also have a working knowledge of the construction and main component parts of the vehicle, its weight, height, width and length. They should make sure it is roadworthy, has sufficient fuel for the test, displays L plates front and rear, has a road tax disc and a secure seat for the examiner. Applicants must bring their full driving licence and provisional PCV driving licence with them and be punctual.

Working knowledge of the vehicle is an EC requirement which is now a formal part of the test. Applicants are required to understand enough about the test vehicle to appreciate when it is unsafe to drive, to be alert to possible defects, and to be able to report verbally or in writing to a fitter or mechanic the repairs thought to be needed.

A driver may drive a PCV without supervision immediately on the strength of a pass certificate and the provisional entitlement.

Documents Required for Tests

Applicants must first pass the theory test and when attending for this the following documents must be produced.
1. An appropriate licence for the category of vehicle for which the test is required.
2. Evidence of identity, ie passport, cheque or credit cards, etc (provided they bear a signature and a photograph of the applicant).

On the successful completion of this test the applicant, when presenting him or herself for the practical test, must supply:
- (a) a theory test "pass" certificate
- (b) an appropriate licence (as mentioned above)
- (c) evidence of identity (as mentioned above)
- (d) an appropriate vehicle in which the test is to be conducted.

The applicant must declare on the Driving Test Report form that the vehicle provided for the test is covered against third party risk insurance.

Badges

There is no longer any requirement for drivers to wear PSV licence number badges.

Minimum Ages of Drivers

Currently the normal minimum age of drivers of buses is 21, but drivers aged 18 or more with provisional Category "D" or "D1" entitlement, may drive category D or D1 vehicles as a properly supervised trainee, whilst the vehicle is not carrying any passengers or whilst taking a driving test.

Holders of full Cat D licences and who are aged 18 years or over may drive a PCV used under a PSV Operator's Licence, ss.19 or 22 permits (see *Permits*) with passengers, provided the bus is on a regular service where the route length is 50km or less or the vehicle is constructed to carry not more than 16 passengers and the journey is within the United Kingdom provided they hold the appropriate driving entitlement. Such drivers may drive empty PCVs without any restriction.

From September 2008 onwards, the age of 20 years will be substituted for the current age of 21 years and only new drivers who have passed the initial CPC test will be able to drive from age 18 years under the 50km route length rule.

Disciplinary Powers of Traffic Commissioners

Traffic Commissioners retain disciplinary powers over PSV drivers. Schedule 2 of the **Road Traffic (Driver Licensing and Information Systems) Act 1989** allows for the referral by the Secretary of State for Transport of questions relating to the conduct of applicants for, or holders of, the PCV entitlement to the Traffic Commissioner, and where the Commissioner notifies the Secretary of State that the applicant or holder is not in his opinion a fit person to hold the entitlement, the Secretary of State must refuse to grant a licence, revoke or suspend the licence or disqualify the holder indefinitely or for a determined period.

Appeals against the refusal of the Secretary of State to reconsider refusing an applicant a licence, revoking or suspending a PCV entitlement or disqualifying a PCV driver can still be made to a Magistrate's Court (Sheriff's Court in Scotland), and any Traffic Commissioner to whom the matter was referred then becomes the respondent in the case. PCV drivers must declare all convictions to their local Area Traffic Office.

A Traffic Commissioner may also determine that a driver may only drive a PCV as a provisional category D licence holder until he passes a category D re-test.

Offences

A person who drives a passenger carrying vehicle on the road without being in possession of the appropriate driving entitlement commits an offence. Also an employer who employs such a person for this purpose can be prosecuted. In both cases a fine on summary conviction can be imposed.

Endorsement and Disqualification

A disqualification by the courts from holding a category B entitlement will automatically disqualify the holder from driving a category D or D1 vehicle.

A PCV driver disqualified from holding a D or D1 entitlement will not automatically be debarred from holding a category B entitlement.

Unified driving licences (the pink part of the licence) do not contain statements of provisional driving licence entitlements or particulars of convictions, penalty points, endorsements and disqualifications — these are entered on a technically "separate" document (the green part) issued with the licence and known as the counterpart.

Duration

Currently category D/D1 entitlements are normally valid until age 45, or for five years if newly issued to someone over 40.

Note: This will not apply to new PCV licences issued after the Third EC Directive on Driving Licences comes into effect in 2008.

Renewals thereafter are every five years up to age 65, and then annually.

Medical reports are required at each renewal.

Maintenance Staff

Staff who have held category C driving entitlement for at least two years may drive a category D vehicle in the following circumstances:

(a) the vehicle is damaged or is defective and is being driven to a place for repairs,
(b) the vehicle is being road tested after having been repaired.

The vehicle must not carry people who have no connection with the operator.

Holders of full category D licences may drive a passenger carrying vehicle recovery vehicle (not articulated) up to 10.2 tonnes ULW.

Preserved Buses

Preserved or historic buses, defined as buses more than 30 years old, may be driven by the holder of a category B licence provided he or she is age 21 or over, the vehicle is not carrying more than eight passengers and is not being used for hire or reward.

Grandfather Rights

Drivers who hold a "Restricted" category D entitlement may drive large PCVs provided such vehicles are not used for hire or reward.

This restricted entitlement was only available to drivers who applied before 1 October 1992.

PCV Driving Entitlement Changes

The changes in PCV driving entitlements in 1991 and 1997 are summarised in the following table:

Vehicle	Old category/sub-category	Corresponding new category/sub-category
Small passenger carrying vehicle (9 to 16 passenger seats) not used for hire or reward	D1	D1 (not for hire or reward)

used for hire or reward	D limited to 16 passenger seats	D1

Passenger carrying vehicle
    9 or more passenger seats
    9 or more passenger seats, up to 5.5 metres long
 	
17 or more passenger seats not used for "hire or reward"
	D
	
	D (not more than 5.5 metres long)
	
	Restricted D
		D
		
		D1 plus vehicle in category D not more than 5.5 metres long
		
		Vehicles in category D not used for "hire or reward"

Vehicle drawing a trailer more than 750kg	D+E	D+E

4 CONDITION OF VEHICLES

CONSTRUCTION AND USE REGULATIONS

The **Motor Vehicles (Construction and Use) Regulations 1986** (SI 1986 No. 1078) as amended apply to all motor vehicles, both goods and passenger. Different types of vehicle are defined in the regulations, as listed below.

Definitions

Motor vehicle
A mechanically propelled vehicle intended or adapted for use on the roads.

Motor car and heavy motor car
A motor car is a mechanically propelled vehicle (excluding a motorcycle or invalid carriage) constructed to carry a load or passengers.

If the vehicle is a passenger vehicle it will be classed as a motor car if its unladen weight does not exceed 3050kg and it is adapted to carry not more than seven passengers.

A *heavy motor car* is a vehicle constructed to carry a load or up to eight passengers and exceeds 2540kg unladen weight.

Bus
A motor vehicle constructed or adapted to carry more than eight seated passengers in addition to the driver.

Articulated bus
A bus so constructed that it can be divided (but only by using workshop facilities) into two vehicles, one of which is a motor vehicle and passengers can at all times pass from one part to another.

Large bus
A vehicle constructed or adapted to carry 17 or more seated passengers in addition to the driver.

Coach
A large bus with a maximum gross weight of more than 7.5 tonnes and a maximum speed exceeding 60 mph.

Minibus
A motor vehicle constructed or adapted to carry more than 8 but not more than 16 seated passengers.

Trailer
A vehicle drawn by a motor vehicle but excluding any part of an articulated bus.

Close-coupled
In relation to a trailer this means that the wheels on each side remain parallel to the longitudinal axis of the trailer when in motion and the centre of their respective areas of contact with the road does not exceed 1m.

Dual-purpose vehicle
A vehicle constructed or adapted for the carriage both of passengers and of goods or burden of any description, with an unladen weight not exceeding 2040kg and which either is capable of all-wheel drive or meets the following requirements as to body construction:
    (a) it must have a permanently fitted rigid roof, with or without a sliding panel
    (b) the area to the rear of the driver's seat must:
        (i) be permanently fitted with at least one row of upholstered transverse seats (fixed or folding) for two or more passengers, and
        (ii) have windows, of either glass or other transparent material, at side and rear. The area or aggregate area of light on each side must be not less than 1850cm^2 and at the rear not less than 770cm^2

(c) the distance between the rearmost part of the steering wheel and the back rests of the row of transverse seats satisfying the requirements specified under (b)(i) above (or, if there is more than one such row of seats, the distance to the rearmost such row) must, when the seats are ready for use, be not less than one-third of the distance between the rearmost part of the steering wheel and the rearmost part of the floor of the vehicle.

First used

Any provision applicable to a motor vehicle first used on or after a specified date need not apply to that vehicle if it was manufactured at least six months before the date.

Maximum Laden Weights

The maximum authorised weight of a loaded bus with two axles is 18 tonnes (18,000kg). The maximum authorised weight for a bus with three axles is 25,000kg and 30,000kg if four axles (26,000kg and 32,000kg respectively if fitted with "road friendly suspension", eg air suspension). Articulated buses may gross 28,000kg. These weights are as measured on the road and include water, oil, fuel, driver, passengers and luggage. The maximum drive axle weight is 11,500kg. Some vehicles, particularly smaller ones, have lower design weights than these authorised maximum values.

It is most important that a vehicle does not exceed any of its maximum gross or axle weights shown on the manufacturer's plate. If it does, it is an absolute offence which will attract a fixed penalty and licence (points) endorsements for the driver. If the authorities find a vehicle on the road overweight a prosecution will almost always follow and this can result in both the driver and the operator being heavily fined and being called to appear before the Traffic Commissioners.

The problems of overweight can occur in a number of ways, eg badly stowed luggage, passengers on trips to the continent taking advantage of lower priced goods such as wines, beers and spirits and "stocking up" before making the return trip, etc.

Whilst the operator should advise passengers of the constraints on the amount of baggage they can carry, the driver should also remind them of these limits, especially in the second example given above, as any surplus may have to be jettisoned if the police or an examiner from the Vehicle and Operator Services Agency (VOSA) decide to check weigh the vehicle. If the coach is found overweight the police, etc will require the excess to be offloaded before allowing it to proceed.

Maximum Dimensions of Buses and Coaches

The designs of PSVs are progressively reflecting the differing operational requirements between luxury or commuter coaches and scheduled and registered bus services, recognising the public's desire for greater accessibility in such vehicles. Either UK or EU regulations can be used to meet the needs of the vehicle operator and his or her passengers.

The overall maximum length for a non-articulated bus is 13.5 metres on two axles and 15 metres on three or more axles. A bus towing a trailer or an articulated bus must not exceed 18.75m.

Maximum height is 4.57m, but is limited to 4m when going on an international journey. Maximum width is 2.55m (excluding any guide wheels not projecting sideways more than 75mm).

Manufacturer's Plates

Every bus, including articulated buses, first used on or after 1 April 1982 must be fitted with a manufacturer's plate containing the following particulars:
– manufacturer's name
– vehicle type

- engine type and power
- chassis or serial number
- number of axles
- maximum axle weight for each axle
- maximum gross weight
- maximum train weight
- maximum weight in Great Britain for each axle
- maximum gross weight in Great Britain.

Twin Wheels

Twin wheels are regarded as one wheel if their centres of contact with the road are less than 460mm apart.

Speedometers

These must be fitted to all motor vehicles registered from 1 October 1937. Requirements for accuracy apply to speedometers incorporated in analogue type tachographs, which are required to operate within certain tolerances.

Vehicles first used from 1 April 1984 must be fitted with an instrument which allows the speed indication to be read in both mph and kph either simultaneously or, by the operation of a switch, separately.

Vehicles limited by either law or their construction to a speed not exceeding 25mph do not require speedometers.

Speedometers must be maintained in good working order at all "material times", ie when a vehicle is used on a journey unless:
  (a) a defect occurs during a journey, or
  (b) following a defect, steps are taken to have the equipment repaired or replaced as soon as possible.

Drivers should report any vehicle where the speedometer is:
  (a) not fitted
  (b) inoperative
  (c) not illuminated
  (d) not visible to the driver, or
  (e) where it has a broken or missing dial glass.

The requirement to fit speedometers does not extend to vehicles fitted with EC-approved analogue tachograph recording equipment, as such instruments include speedometers.

Speed Limiters

Every coach exceeding a gross vehicle weight of 7.5 tonnes first used between 1 April 1974 and 31 December 1987 must be fitted with a speed limiter if it would otherwise be capable of exceeding 70mph. The limiter for these vehicles must be set at or below 70mph.

Buses and coaches first used between 1 January 1988 and 1 January 2005, with a maximum gross weight exceeding 10.0 tonnes and capable of a speed exceeding 100kph must be fitted with a speed limiter calibrated to a set speed not exceeding 100kph.

Buses and coaches first used between 1 October 2001 and 31 December 2004, with a maximum gross vehicle weight between 7.5 tonnes and 10.0 tonnes and capable of a speed exceeding 100kph must be fitted with a speed limiter calibrated to enable a stabilised speed not exceeding 100kph.

Since 1 January 2005 all new* buses and coaches, irrespective of weight or form of fuel, must be fitted with a speed limiter enabling a stabilised speed not exceeding 100kph.

*Vehicles with a maximum gross vehicle weight not exceeding 5 tonnes used solely for national transport operations have until 1 January 2008 to comply.

Speed limiters must be sealed to prevent their being tampered with and the vehicle must display a plate in a conspicuous position in the driving compartment clearly marked with the set speed.

Tachographs

In accordance with EU regulations tachographs must be fitted to all vehicles adapted or constructed for the commercial carriage of more than 9 persons, including the driver. Such vehicles first registered after 1 May 2006 must be fitted with a digital tachograph. (For more detailed information on tachographs, see *The Tachograph*.)

Warning Devices

Buses and coaches having an overall travelling height exceeding *3m* must have either:

(a) a notice displayed in a prominent position in the driving compartment showing the overall travelling height of the vehicle, or

(b) documents such as a map, or maps, within easy reach of the driver giving details of the route, or choice of routes which can be taken, to eliminate the risk of the vehicle striking bridges or other overhead structures during the course of the journey.

If (a) is adopted the notice must show the overall travelling height in feet and inches, or in both feet and inches and in metres; the numbers used for giving the height in feet and inches must be at least 40mm tall and those giving this information in feet and inches and metres must not differ by more than 50mm.

The total height shown in the notice must be not less than the travelling height of the vehicle nor more than 150mm above that height.

Television Sets

Television receiving apparatus may not be installed in a motor vehicle if the screen is partly or wholly visible to the driver (either directly or reflected) whilst driving the vehicle, unless it is only capable of displaying information:

(a) about the state of the vehicle or its equipment
(b) about the location of the vehicle on the road
(c) to assist the driver in seeing the road adjacent to the vehicle
(d) to enable the driver to monitor passenger safety at the centre entrance/exit doors
(e) to assist the driver in reaching the destination.

Note: (b) and (c) taken together effectively legalise closed circuit TV reversing devices.

Receiving monitors and videos

"Television receiving apparatus" is defined as a cathode ray tube on which can be displayed an image derived from a television broadcast, a recording, camera or computer.

Performing rights

If recorded music or image equipment is to be played in a coach (either by radio, television or video), licences must be obtained by the operator. Details are available from the Performing Rights Society, 29–33 Berners Street, London W1P 4AA (tel: 020 7580 5544).

A scale of fees applies in respect of each coach with equipment installed (equipment can be transferred between coaches).

Mirrors

All passenger and dual-purpose vehicles must have at least three rear-view mirrors, two fitted externally — one on the offside and the other on the nearside — and the third internally (unless a mirror so fitted would be inadequate) to show traffic to the rear and both sides rearwards. On all vehicles registered from 1.4.69 the edges of the internal mirror must be covered by a protective material.

On all vehicles registered after 1 June 1978 both the offside mirror and internal mirror must be capable of adjustment from the driving seat.

Vehicles over 3.5 tonnes maximum gross weight must be fitted with "close-proximity" external mirrors giving a view of both rearward approaching and overtaking traffic.

Each exterior rear view mirror must be visible to the driver either through a side window or through the part of the windscreen swept by the wiper. Drivers should ensure that their mirrors are always clean and correctly positioned to give immediate viewing from the driving position.

All minibuses first used from 1 April 1988 must be fitted with rear view mirrors or other means (for example where a rear door is used as a service door, a rear view lens) to enable a seated driver to see the area immediately outside a service door. This requirement is deemed to be met if a driver can see a child 1.3m high standing 1m behind his vehicle.

Safety Glass

Passenger and dual-purpose vehicles first used on or after 1 January 1959 must have safety glass fitted to the windscreen and all windows on the outside of the vehicle.

The safety glass fitted to the windscreen and all windows wholly or partly in front of and on either side of the driver's seat of motor vehicles manufactured from 1 December 1977 and first used from 1 June 1978 must conform to specifications BS857 or BS5282. The "safety glass" fitted to other windows of a bus (including minibuses) may be *safety glazing* provided that the windows do not:
  (a) face the rear of the vehicle and
  (b) form the whole or part of a door giving access to the exterior of the vehicle.

Partitions (ie transverse glass windows or panels) not made of safety glass are permissible provided that they are adequately protected against the likelihood of breakage by passengers being thrown against them.

Whilst safety glass is desirable for windows on the upper deck of buses, it is mandatory for vehicles manufactured on or after 1 October 1981.

Windscreens and windows should be kept clean to ensure a clear view of the road and other traffic.

Windscreen Wipers and Washers

An efficient automatic windscreen wiper or wipers must be fitted to every vehicle from which an adequate view to the front cannot be obtained other than through the windscreen.

Wipers must be capable of ensuring the driver an adequate view of the road to the front and the front of the near and offsides. Such vehicles, unless they are being used to provide a local service or on a journey incidental to such use, must also be fitted with a windscreen washer which, in conjunction with the wiper, can keep the screen clear of mud, etc.

Horns and Reversing Alarms

Every motor vehicle must be fitted with an instrument capable of giving audible and sufficient warning of its approach or position. Only a vehicle used on official emergency services may be fitted with a gong, bell siren, two-tone horn or instrument capable of emitting a similar sound.

A reversing alarm may be fitted to a bus, provided the sound emitted by the alarm is different to that which is employed at "pelican" pedestrian crossings.

Reversing alarms and horns may not be sounded when the vehicle is stationary on a road nor when it is in motion on a restricted road at night between the hours of 23.30 and 07.00, except in an emergency. Horns may be sounded on a stationary vehicle:

(a) to warn of the presence to or of another moving vehicle on or near the road
(b) to raise the alarm as to theft of the vehicle or its contents
(c) on a bus to summon assistance for the driver, conductor or inspector.

Fuel Tanks

Motor vehicle fuel tanks must be so maintained that they are reasonably secure against damage and are free from leakages. Motor vehicles first used from 1 July 1973 must be equipped with metal fuel tanks but this requirement does not apply where the vehicle is legibly and indelibly marked with a designated approval mark indicating that the vehicle has been approved in respect of fire risks.

Radio Interference Suppression

Petrol engined vehicles first used from 1 April 1974 must be fitted with radio interference suppression equipment and be clearly marked with the designated approval mark for this equipment.

Smoke and Emissions

Every motor vehicle must be so constructed that no avoidable smoke or visible vapour is emitted. Excess fuel devices must not be used on diesel engine vehicles whilst in action.

It is an offence to drive a vehicle which is emitting smoke or dangerous vapour.

Specific standards have progressively applied to buses and coaches first registered on or after:

1 October 1993   "EURO" standard No. 1
1 October 1996   "EURO" standard No. 2
1 October 2001   "EURO" standard No. 3
1 October 2006   "EURO" standard No. 4

"EURO" standard No. 5 will apply to buses and coaches first registered on or after 1 October 2009.

Vehicles adapted to qualify for the higher standards, by having equipment such as a particular trap fitted to prevent the emission of solid matter, may allow an operator to claim a Reduced Pollution Certificate for the vehicle — enabling payment reduction on Vehicle Excise Duty.

Low Emission Zones (LEZ)

Local authorities have powers to impose minimum "EURO" emission standards on vehicles entering a defined area and to make charges on vehicles which do not meet the set minimum standard. The City of London is likely to be the first authority to introduce a (LEZ) zone when the London scheme commences (applicable to buses and coaches) in July 2008 and minibuses in 2010.

Tyres

It is illegal to use a tyre:

(a) which is not correctly inflated

(b) which has a break in its fabric or a cut in excess of 25mm or 10% of the section width of the tyres, deep enough to reach the body cords

(c) which has a lump, bulge or tear caused by separation, etc

(d) which is the wrong size or type for the vehicle's use

(e) which has any portion of ply or cord exposed

(f) on which the base of any groove which showed in the original tread pattern is not clearly visible

(g) on which either:

    (i) the grooves of the tread pattern do not have a depth of at least 1mm throughout a continuous band measuring at least ¾ of the breadth of tread and round the entire outer circumference of the tyre, or

    (ii) where the original tread pattern did not extend beyond ¾ of the breadth of the tread, the base of any groove which showed in the tyre's original tread pattern does not have a depth of at least 1mm.

Note: The grooves of the tread pattern of tyres fitted to passenger vehicles with up to nine seats, goods vehicles not exceeding 3500kg maximum gross weight and light trailers, must be a minimum of 1.6mm in depth throughout a continuous band situated in the central three quarters of the breadth of tread and round the entire outer circumference of the tyre.

"Breadth of tread" means the breadth of that part of the tyre which is in contact with the road under normal conditions of use measured at 90° to the peripheral line of the tread. "Tread pattern" means the combination of plain surfaces and grooves extending across the breadth of the tread and round the entire outer circumference of the tyres excluding:

(i) any tie-bars or tread wear indicators
(ii) any features which are designed to wear out substantially before the rest of the pattern under normal conditions of use, and
(iii) any other minor features.

"Tie-bars" means any part of the tyre moulded in the tread pattern of the tyre for the purpose of bracing two or more features of such tread pattern.

"Tread wear indicators" means any bar, not being a tiebar, projecting from the base of the tread pattern and moulded between two or more features of the tyre's tread pattern for the purpose of indicating the extent of wear of such a tread pattern.

Points (a), (b) and (e) above do not apply where the tyre and wheel to which it is fitted are so constructed that when running deflated the tyre will operate safely and its outside wall bears an identifying mark to that effect.

These regulations do not apply to a broken down vehicle or a vehicle being taken to a place to be broken up where in either case it is being towed by a vehicle not exceeding 20mph.

Passenger vehicles seating up to eight persons *but not buses*, may carry specially compact temporary spare wheels/tyres provided that when used the speed of the vehicle does not exceed 50mph.

Recut pneumatic tyres must not be used if the ply or cord has been cut or exposed by the recutting process or it has been wholly or partially recut in a different pattern to that of the manufacturer's recut tread pattern.

It is also illegal to fit to motor vehicles having only two axles and equipped with one or two single wheels, tyres of different types, ie cross-ply, radial or bias-belted, in the following manners:

(a) diagonal-ply tyres or bias-belted tyres on the rear axle and radial-ply tyres on the front axle, or

(b) diagonal-ply tyres on the rear axle and bias-belted tyres on the front axle.

This does not apply if wide tyres, other than those used for engineering plant, are fitted.

Also, tyres of different structures must not be fitted to vehicles with:

(a) more than one steerable axle, or
(b) more than one driven axle not being a steerable axle.

Maintenance of tyres

Although maintenance of tyres, like total vehicle maintenance is the responsibility of the maintenance staff, there are certain periodical checks that are the responsibility of the driver.

The following daily check-list is therefore recommended:

(a) check tyre pressures (cold). Tyres generate heat during running and more so during hot weather, which may cause pressures to rise some 10–15 pounds above the recommended pressure
(b) examine tyres for cuts, blisters and stones, etc especially between twin tyres. At first sight any of these may not appear to be dangerous, but they may become so in the course of a journey
(c) check twin rear tyres. Inner and outer tyres should have the same diameters and the same pressures. One twin tyre below pressure will cause overloading of the other and an eventual blow-out
(d) make sure that all tyres show a reasonable amount of tread pattern and that the spare wheel and tyre are in similar good order and inflated to the correct pressure.

Tyre service and supply

For the benefit of operators or owner-drivers, the tyre manufacturers and their distributors offer substantial repair and replacement facilities.

Check the Yellow Pages or other sources for your nearest supplier.

Tyre loads and speed ratings

Vehicles must be fitted with tyres designed to support their maximum axle weights when driven at the maximum legal speed limits.

The tyres of a bus used to provide a local service may carry up to 110% of the maximum load normally permitted for those tyres when the bus concerned is driven at speeds not exceeding 50mph.

Doors

It is an offence to open the door of a vehicle when the vehicle is moving or when this may cause injury or damage to any person.

Seat Belts and Anchorage Points

The exact requirement for seat belts and anchorage points depends on the type of vehicle, its weight and date of first use. Generally all cars, passenger or dual-purpose vehicles constructed to carry 12 or fewer people (excluding the driver), minibuses under 3500kg, and certain light goods vehicles under 3500kg must be provided with seat belts and anchorage points for the driver's seat and front passenger seats (either all seats or a "specified" seat, eg the one next to the driver).

This "basic" requirement was extended to all "exposed" forward-facing seats of coaches first used on or after 1 October 1988, and still further in 2001 when seat belts were required at all forward and rearward facing seats of all non-urban buses first used on or after 1 October 2001. These fitting requirements are independent of the use requirement for minibuses and coaches carrying children (see later).

The fitting of seats with integral seat belts, anchorage points and built-in seat belts is allowed as an alternative to conventional seat belt anchorage points and seat belts.

Some vehicle types first used from 1 April 1973 must be fitted with seat belts which can be put on with one hand and which must be easy to adjust and stow. The stowing device must prevent the belt from lying on the floor.

Seat belts *and* anchorage points must be maintained in a proper condition at all times so that the belt, its achorages, fastenings and adjusting device are free from any obvious defects which would seriously affect the proper functioning of the seat belt in the event of an accident. Anchorage points and all load bearing parts of the vehicle's structure or panelling within 30cm of each anchorage point must at all times be free from serious corrosion, distortion or fracture.

All passenger vehicles with nine or fewer seats, including the driver's, must have seat belt anchorage points which comply with EU requirements for every forward facing seat. The same EU standard applies to all anchorage points fitted after 1 October 2001.

Rear seat belts

Cars and dual-purpose vehicles first used on or after 1 January 1987 must be fitted with rear seat belts as follows:

(a) vehicles with not more than two forward facing seats behind the driver's seat:
  (i) an inertia reel belt for at least one seat, or
  (ii) a three-point, lap, or disabled person's belt or child restraint for each seat
(b) vehicles with more than two (ie up to six) forward facing seats behind the driver's seat:
  (i) an inertia reel belt for one outboard seat and a three-point, lap or disabled person's belt for at least one other seat, or
  (ii) a three-point belt for one seat and either a child restraint or disabled person's belt for at least one other seat. (One of the two seats fitted must be an outboard seat) or
  (iii) a three-point, lap or disabled person's belt or child restraint for each of those seats.

Seat Belts on Buses Carrying Children

Seat belts are required to be fitted to forward-facing seats in minibuses and coaches carrying all children (not just school children) aged under 16 whenever a group of three or more children are on an "organised trip" and where the journey is made for the purpose of the trip, ie it is used specifically where the transport of children is central to the purpose of the journey.

The regulations do not apply where the children are travelling on a vehicle used to provide a registered service (so long as it is not an excursion or tour) or a service provided under a London Local Service Licence or on behalf of LRT where 50% or more of the seats are available to the general public or services used "wholly or mainly to provide a transport service for the general public", even if these incidentally allow some child passengers to make an "organised trip" as defined above.

3 for 2 concession

The concession under which three seated children of 14 or under count as two children for the purpose of carrying capacity is qualified so that it only applies if none are occupying seats fitted with belts.

Wearing of Seat Belts

Drivers and front seat passengers (ie those seated alongside the driver) of all vehicles must wear the seat belts provided.

Exemptions from these requirements are given for specific people, including:
   (a) the driver when reversing a vehicle
   (b) a driving instructor (as defined in the driving licences regulations) whilst supervising a learner driver in a manoeuvre which includes reversing
   (c) the holder of a certificate signed by a registered medical practitioner, exempting him or her from wearing seat belts, on medical grounds
   (d) a constable protecting or escorting another person
   (e) a prison officer protecting or escorting another person
   (f) firemen

(g) a taxi driver whilst seeking hire, answering a call for hire, or carrying a passenger for hire, or the driver of a private hire vehicle whilst the vehicle is being used to carry a passenger for hire

(h) a qualified tester who is conducting a person in a driving test and who, by wearing a seat belt, would endanger him or herself or any other person

(i) a person occupying a seat where the seat belt either does not conform to the Construction and Use Regulations, or has an inertia reel mechanism which is locked because the vehicle is on, or has been on, a steep incline

(j) a person riding in a vehicle under trade plates whilst investigating or remedying a mechanical fault in the vehicle.

It is the responsibility of the individual to wear the seat belt but responsibility rests with the driver when a child under the age of 14 is being carried in the front seat of any vehicle with a GVW of less than 3.5 tonnes.

Children under the age of 14 carried in the rear seat of any motor car (excluding a taxi) must wear any "available" seat belts.

Fines can be imposed where these regulations are not complied with.

There is no lower age limit for these regulations but if the passenger is under 14 he or she will not be allowed in the middle front passenger seat without an approved seat belt (it is illegal to carry an unrestrained child in the front seat of virtually any vehicle). Children over one year old may use an adult seat belt or other approved device, unless they are disabled, when they may use any specially designed and constructed seat belt. Disabled adults must use a standard seat belt unless they are in a specially constructed or adapted vehicle, when they may use any seat belt specially designed for them.

Trailers

Maximum laden weights
The maximum laden weight of a trailer manufactured before 27 February 1977, with only a parking brake and brakes which operate automatically on overrun of the trailer is 3560kg. For trailers manufactured from 27 February 1977 with brakes that operate automatically on overrun and irrespective of any other brakes, the maximum laden weight is 3500kg.

The laden weight of an unbraked trailer used on the road must not exceed its maximum gross weight. It may only be towed by a vehicle whose kerbside weight is at least double the unladen weight of the trailer together with the weight of any load the trailer is carrying.

Trailers under 750kg gross weight must be fitted with brakes if their laden weight exceeds half the towing vehicle's weight.

Unbraked trailers (markings)
Every unbraked trailer must be marked in a conspicuous and readily accessible position on the left or nearside with its maximum gross weight (in kg).

Detached trailers
When detached from the drawing vehicle a trailer must be prevented from moving by the use of a brake, chain, chock or other efficient device applied to at least one of its wheels.

Length of tow rope
Where a motor vehicle is drawing a trailer by means of a tow rope or chain the distance between their nearest points must not exceed 4.5m. Where the distance exceeds 1.5m the tow rope or chain must be made clearly visible from both sides. No limit of length is stated for a rigid tow bar.

Carriage of passengers in trailers

PSV (Construction and Use) Regulations prohibit the use of trailers for the conveyance of passengers for hire or reward. Broken down vehicles carrying passengers may be towed provided they are not drawn faster than 30mph and the vehicles are attached by a rigid draw bar.

PSVs drawing trailers

A bus or coach must not draw a trailer unless:
  (a) it is an empty bus drawing another empty bus which has broken down, or
  (b) it is a trailer and the overall length of the combination does not exceed 18.75m.

No trailer may, in any circumstances, be drawn by an articulated bus.

Vehicles with rear exits are prohibited from drawing any trailers. Whilst passengers are being carried by a vehicle no person must cause or permit any unnecessary obstruction to any entrance, exit or gangway of the vehicle.

This means that if the vehicle has a rear exit a trailer *must not* be attached.

Passengers must not be carried in a trailer used for hire or reward unless it is a broken down bus towed at a speed less than 30mph by a rigid draw bar.

Note: The small motorised "road trains" often used in tourist areas are not PSVs.

Brakes

The Construction and Use Regulations lay down specific requirements for the design, application and maintenance of brakes. They do so, in most cases, by applying the requirements of EC Directive 79/489 EC (as amended).

Every passenger vehicle and trailer (except small trailers with total axle weights not exceeding 750kg) first used on or after 1 April 1983 must comply with the EC directive. Vehicles first used before that date may also comply with the directive or may comply with the Construction and Use Regulations. There is some slight relaxation in braking criteria for vehicles registered before 1 January 1968.

Parking brake

Every passenger vehicle must have a parking brake which is independent of the main brakes and capable, by direct mechanical action, of holding the vehicle stationary on a gradient of at least 16% (ie 1 in 6.25). If the vehicle is required to meet EU braking standards its parking brake must be capable of holding it with an *unbraked* trailer attached on a gradient of 12% (1 in 8.33). A spring brake can be considered to be a mechanical means of action.

Main and secondary brakes

Every passenger vehicle's braking system must have a main means of operation (ie the footbrake) and a secondary means, which could be an emergency brake or a dual system, the "split" part of which is also operated by the footbrake. If one half of the braking system fails, the remainder must continue to operate with the required residual efficiency. In the case of a vehicle with a dual braking system the parking brake must be able to operate with the vehicle in motion unless it is a transmission brake.

Retarders

Use may be made of a retarder to assist a vehicle to comply with EU braking specifications on downhill speed control and brake fade, but no account may be taken of the contribution of the retarder to assist in complying with the braking efficiencies referred to below.

Antilock Braking System (ABS)

A coach over 12t gross weight first used on or after 1 April 1992 must be equipped with a category 1 (individual wheel) anti-lock brake system. This requirement extends to new buses first used on or after 1 May 2002.

A vehicle developing a failure in its ABS may be driven to complete its journey and/or to a place of repair *provided* the brakes otherwise comply with construction and use regulations.

Braking efficiencies

The general minimum braking efficiencies for vehicles to which the regulations apply are as follows:

	Minimum (%) Parking brake	Braking Main brake	Efficiencies Secondary brake
Passenger vehicles complying with the EC directive and first used:			
on or after 1 April 1983:	16	50	25
drawing a trailer:	12	45	25

Application of trailer brakes

The driver must be able to operate the brakes of both the motor vehicle and its trailer, except where the trailer is fitted with an overrun brake, or the trailer is a broken down vehicle being towed in such a manner that it cannot be steered by its own steering gear.

Turning Circles (Swept Circle) and Cut Out

All buses registered in the UK since 9 March 2005 have had to meet the turning circle requirements as set out in EU Directive 96/53 (as amended by EU Directive 2002/7) instead of the previously applicable UK Construction and Use Regulations (see diagrams below).

Cut out (out swing)

When moving forward from a straight line position where the nearside front corner of the vehicle is positioned on the outer of the two circles shown in the diagram below, to turn in a clockwise direction, no part of the vehicle shall move outside of the vertical plane by more than 0.6m.

Turning Circle

Turning Circle
The vehicle has to manoeuvre between 2 concentric circles of 12.5 metres and 5.3 metres radius

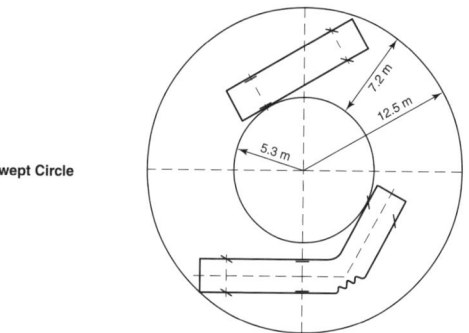

Swept Circle

Cut Out (Out-swing)

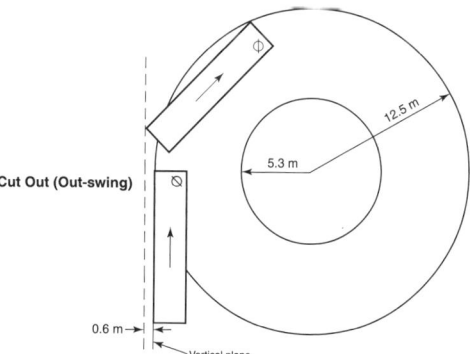

Cut Out (Out-swing)

Reproduced with the kind permission of VOSA.

Articulated Buses

The test is the same for articulated vehicles except that the two rigid portions of the vehicle must be aligned with the vertical plane before moving in the clockwise direction.

Roof Strength of Coaches

All single deck "high floor" (ie with below deck luggage lockers) coaches first used on or after 1 April 1993 must comply with ECE Regulation 66 requiring sufficient roof strength to provide a passenger survival space in a "roll-over" accident.

Noise

No motor vehicle or trailer which causes excessive noise may be used on the road, nor may it be used in a manner to cause excessive noise which could be avoided.

Noise or excessive noise emitted by a vehicle includes that emitted by an inefficient exhaust silencer device.

LIGHTING

Between sunset and sunrise (and during periods of seriously reduced visibility) all vehicles are required to carry two front lamps showing white to the front, two rear position lamps showing red to the rear, two red "retro" reflectors, a rear registration plate lamp and end outline marker lamps (if applicable). Buses also require two headlamps but for those first used before 1 October 1969 only one need be a dipped beam lamp.

Restrictions

1. *A red light must not* be shown to the front of a vehicle.
2. *A white light must not* be shown to the rear of a vehicle except in the following circumstances:
   (a) for the purpose of reversing
   (b) in order to illuminate the interior of a vehicle
   (c) to illuminate the rear number plate
   (d) to illuminate a PSV destination board or a taxi meter.

Special provisions do permit the use of blue, amber or green lights on fire, ambulance, or police service vehicles, medical practitioners' vehicles and special service vehicles.

Use of headlamps and auxiliary lamps

Headlamps must be used during the hours of darkness in all unlit areas (or where the street lamps are more than 200 yards apart). "Hours of darkness" is usually defined as half an hour after sunset to half an hour before sunrise.

Both lights must be illuminated together and it is an offence to drive in non-illuminated areas (where street lamps are more than 200 yards apart) with only one headlamp working.

Headlamps must be switched off when the vehicle is stationary except at traffic stops. They must not be fitted more than 1200mm from the ground, nor less than 500mm from the ground.

Headlamps must be fitted with a dipping mechanism to avoid dazzle and no light other than a dipping headlight may be moved, by swivelling or otherwise, while the vehicle is in motion. Every matched pair of headlamps must emit beams of the same colour light. Lamps fitted and used as fog or spotlights must be fitted with a permanently deflected beam. There is no minimum height for these lamps provided they are used only during poor visibility.

Road clearance vehicles and large passenger carrying vehicles first used before 1 October 1969 are permitted to use only one headlamp. A vehicle being towed and a snow plough are exempt from using headlamps.

Front Fog Lamps

In conditions where visibility is seriously reduced, two fog lamps or a fog lamp and a spot lamp may be used instead of headlamps.

Fog lamps may emit either a white or yellow light and must be positioned so that they do not dazzle or cause inconvenience to other road users.

High Intensity Rear Fog Lamps

Rear fog lamps must be fitted to vehicles and trailers first used from 1 April 1980. Either a single or a matched pair of rear fog lamps can be fitted.

Rear fog lamps may only be used in conditions of poor visibility and must be switched *off* as soon as conditions improve. They may *not* be wired through to the vehicle's brake light circuit.

Direction Indicators

All vehicles must be fitted with direction indicators. Indicators can be of the flashing or semaphore type but the latter may only be fitted to vehicles registered before September 1965. Indicators on vehicles first used from September 1965 must show amber both to the front and rear. They must flash at a rate of between 60 and 120 flashes per minute.

Emergency and Other Services' Vehicles

Distinctive lamps emitting blue, amber or green flashing lights are permitted on certain vehicles carrying out emergency or other services.

Ambulances, fire engines, fire salvage vehicles, Forestry Commission or local authority vehicles used for fire fighting, police vehicles, HM Revenue and Customs, blood transfusion service vehicles, bomb disposal, RAF mountain rescue vehicles, HM coastguard or coastguard auxiliary vehicles used for emergencies on or near the coast, NCB mine rescue vehicles, RNLI vehicles used for launching lifeboats and vehicles used for carrying human tissue for transplants, etc are permitted to carry one or more *blue* lamps.

Vehicles used for road clearance; for testing, maintaining, improving, cleansing or watering roads; inspecting, renewing or installing any apparatus in, on, under or over a road; vehicles constructed or adapted for refuse collection; vehicles having a maximum speed not exceeding 25mph; vehicles having an overall width exceeding 2.9m; breakdown vehicles; vehicles authorised by an Order under s.44 of the **Road Traffic Act 1988**, ie special type vehicles or trailers constructed for special purposes, etc are permitted to carry one or more *amber* lights.

Vehicles used by registered medical practitioners registered by the General Medical Council may carry one or more *green* lamps when used in an emergency.

Warning beacons fitted to vehicles used to escort wide loads at speeds in excess of 25mph and vehicles used at airports may emit a *yellow* light.

All such lamps must be fitted so that the centre is at least *1200mm* above the ground and be visible from any point at a reasonable distance from the vehicle. The frequency of the flashing from these lamps must not be less than 60 nor more than 240 equal times per minute and the interval between each flashing must be constant.

The lamps may only be used when the vehicle is being used for the relevant purposes and in the case of a breakdown vehicle the amber lights may only be illuminated when the vehicle is being used in connection with, or near to, an accident or breakdown, or towing a disabled vehicle. Such vehicles are permitted an additional white lamp for illuminating the area of the accident or breakdown but it must be directed so as not to dazzle or inconvenience other road users.

Road clearance vehicles are also permitted to carry an amber reflecting surface to the rear of the vehicle.

Stop Lights, Reversing Lights and Trailer Lights

Stop lights must be fitted to all vehicles and must always be maintained in a clean and efficient working order.

Reversing lights are not compulsory fittings but if fitted to a vehicle they must be maintained in efficient working order.

Trailer and trailer caravan lighting requirements are the same as those applying to motor vehicles with a few exceptions. Trailers which do not have side lamps *must* have front corner lamps.

Use of Hazard Warning Lights

Hazard warning lights may be used only when the vehicle is stationary on any part of the road, for the purpose of warning other drivers that the vehicle is temporarily causing an obstruction *or* whilst travelling on motorways or unrestricted dual carriageways to warn drivers of following vehicles of the need to slow down because of an obstruction ahead. They may also be used by drivers of buses to summon assistance for the driver, conductor or an inspector on the bus, or whilst a bus displaying "school bus" signs is embarking or disembarking children.

Lights Required During Daylight Hours

The law requires vehicles travelling on a road where visibility is seriously reduced to have obligatory lamps switched on, ie side and rear position lamps and either headlamps or a pair of front fog lamps and rear fog lamps.

It should be noted that front and rear fog lamps may *only* be used in conditions where visibility is *seriously reduced* during the day or at night — it is illegal to use them at any other time.

Lights Required on Stationary Vehicles at Night

Passenger vehicles, other than buses (ie with seats for more than eight passengers) may be parked at night on a restricted road (ie within a 30mph zone) *without lights* if:

(a) they are parked with their nearside close to and parallel to the kerb (except when standing in a recognised parking place or on either side of a one way street) *and*

(b) no part of the vehicle is within *10m* of a road junction.

No lights are required on a vehicle if it is parked within the confines of an area outlined by lamps or traffic signs (cones) to prevent the vehicle, etc from being a danger to other road users.

Any vehicle to which a trailer is attached must keep its lights (side lights) on when parked on the road at night.

General Requirements

Headlamps, front and rear fog lamps and reversing lamps (if fitted) must be set so that they do not dazzle or cause inconvenience to other road users. It is also a requirement of the law that all lights and reflectors, including hazard warning lights, are kept clean and in good working order.

Number Plates

Vehicles, including trailers, not exceeding three tons unladen weight, first registered on or after 1 January 1973 must be fitted with reflex-reflecting number plates. Only the background may be made of retro-reflective material and this must be white for the front plate and yellow for the back plate with letters and figures in black on both.

Vehicles first registered before 1 January 1973 may also be fitted with reflex-reflecting number plates as an alternative to the earlier "white on black" number plates.

A trailer (including a broken-down vehicle being towed) must have the registration number of the towing vehicle fitted on the rear of the vehicle on tow.

Vehicles first registered on or after 1 September 2001 must be fitted with plates made of retro-reflecting material — with colour arrangements as above.

VEHICLE CERTIFICATION, APPROVAL, INSPECTION AND ANNUAL TESTING

Whilst manufacturers and operators have the responsibility for the above, brief details are included in this guide since:
- (a) owner-drivers will need the information and
- (b) employee-drivers should be aware of the requirements of the legislation and be able to check that the vehicles they drive comply.

Certification of Initial Fitness

No PSV which is adapted to carry more than eight passengers may be used unless either:
(a) a certifying officer has issued a *Certificate of Initial Fitness*
(b) a certificate has been issued by the Department for Transport approving the vehicle as a *type vehicle* of a particular type and a certifying officer (if he is satisfied that the vehicle complies with prescribed conditions of fitness) has issued a *Certificate of Conformity*
(c) a *type approval certificate* has been issued.

(Passenger vehicles with over eight seats have not yet come within the scope of type approval and neither have trailers.)

Once in service PSVs must be tested annually on the anniversary of their *first registration* (not their Certificate of Initial Fitness date). Recertification is no longer required but the vehicles are subject to a system of prohibition where necessary.

If (a) or (b) is issued before *registration* it must be sent to the Department for Transport so that the registration number of the vehicle can be noted and the certificate returned.

Vehicle Inspections

All motor vehicles, including PSVs, are subject to spot checks, either at the roadside or at an operator's premises.

Authorised police officers and the Department for Transport's Vehicle and Operator Services Agency (VOSA) examiners may, on production of their authority, test or inspect a vehicle on the road. Only a police officer in uniform may require a vehicle to stop on the road although some VOSA officers who have been accredited by the chief constable of the force for their area now have the same powers of stopping a vehicle as does a police officer. They wear a uniform similar to that of a police officer and must display a Community Accreditation badge. It is an offence to obstruct

an authorised examiner, although drivers of motor vehicles which are *not PSVs* may request a deferred test, which may be refused by a police officer if it appears to him or her that:
  (a) because of an accident involving the vehicle a test should be immediately conducted, or
  (b) the vehicle is so defective that it ought not to be allowed to proceed without first being tested.

If an authorised examiner discovers a defect he or she may, in addition to instituting proceedings for a breach of Construction and Use Regulations, serve a defect notice on the owner via the driver (if he or she is not the owner) of the vehicle requiring, within 28 days, a certificate from an MOT testing station "clearing" the defect.

An examiner may drive a vehicle in order to test it. An examiner or police officer in uniform may inspect a motor vehicle on premises provided the consent of the owner of the vehicle and/or premises is obtained, or 48 hours' notice of intended inspection is given (72 hours if notice is sent by recorded delivery).

Inspection of PSVs

The rules relating to inspection of PSVs by authorised police officers or VOSA examiners are stricter than those given above. They may enter premises to conduct tests at any reasonable time, carry out roadside checks, and if necessary detain vehicles to do so. There is no provision to opt for a delayed test. Drivers must give reasonable assistance to authorised police officers and examiners. Vehicle examiners or police officers in uniform may direct a vehicle which is stationary on a road to be taken to any place not more than five miles distant for inspection purposes. Powers to conduct roadside checks (but not fleet inspections) extend to all buses with more than eight seats, even if these are not PSVs.

Following an inspection as above authorised police officers and vehicle examiners have similar, but not identical powers to prohibit the use of the vehicle. Both may issue an immediate prohibition if they consider the vehicle unfit for service, but only a vehicle examiner may issue a delayed prohibition. Prohibitions relating to passenger vehicles cannot be removed until the vehicle has been inspected in accordance with the directions on the prohibition, which can specify a re-test at an official PSV Testing Station or at an operator's premises if tests are conducted there.

The imposition of a prohibition and the use of a vehicle in contravention of a prohibition can have serious consequences for an operator and may even jeopardise the PSV "O" licence. Drivers should immediately report any prohibition received to their employers.

The forms of prohibition in use by the police and VOSA are:

PG9	Prohibition of driving a vehicle on the road (applicable to ALL vehicles)
PG9/ABC	Combined Refusal/Variation and Exemption
PG9A	Variation of terms of a PG9
PG9B	Permitting the movement of a prohibited vehicle to a place of repair under stated conditions
PG9C	Refusal to remove a prohibition
PG9D	Prohibition/variation defect continuation sheet
PG10	Removal of a prohibition
PGDN(35)	Defect notice (where the defect does not warrant prohibition).
TE160	Prohibition of the movement of a vehicle due to overloading

Any PG9 marked (S) means that in the opinion of the inspectors the defect is such as to show a significant failure in the system of Planned Maintenance and is viewed very seriously by the Traffic Commissioner. If the PG9 is marked (X) this indicates that the defect is not maintenance-related.

Drivers (or their employers) are also legally bound to report to the Traffic Commissioner any damage or accident to a PSV which might affect the safety of its operation.

Weighing of Buses, etc

Persons authorized by a Highway Authority, or police constable authorized in writing by a Police Authority or a Chief Officer of Police, may require a person in charge of a bus, etc to allow it or any trailer drawn by it to be weighed or to proceed to a weighbridge for that purpose.

There is no provision for authorised persons to require the bus, etc to be unloaded to ascertain unladen weight.

If, when the vehicle is weighed, it appears to either an authorised person (ie a Trading Standards officer or police constable) or vehicle examiner that the Construction and Use limits as to the weight of the vehicle have been exceeded or that by reasons of excess overall weight or excess axle weight the driving of the vehicle would involve danger or injury to any person, any of the above authorised persons may serve a notice (TE160) in writing prohibiting the driving of the overweight vehicle on the road until:

- the weight has been reduced, and
- official notice has been given to the person in charge of the vehicle that it is permitted to proceed.

Removal of a prohibition may be withheld until the vehicle has been re-weighed and, for this purpose, the authorised persons or vehicle examiner may give a direction in writing requiring the removal of the vehicle to a specified place subject to any conditions in the direction. Driving the vehicle under such a direction whilst overweight will not be an offence.

If the vehicle is removed over five miles and is found not to be overweight the operator may claim compensation.

Vehicle Testing

Tests of passenger vehicles, including most PSVs and taxis, are carried out annually after their first examination (which is usually conducted on or before the first anniversary of their registration).

The only exception to this rule is the *three year Class IV MOT test* which applies to passenger vehicles with eight or fewer passenger seats (including such vehicles used as a PSV unless they have a CIF). Also within the scope of the *Class IV MOT test* are passenger vehicles with more than eight but fewer than 13 passenger seats but these have to be tested annually after one year. Class IV tests are usually carried out by an authorised examiner (ie private garages franchised for this purpose by the DfT) but may also be carried out by designated councils (ie County or District councils authorised for this purpose by the DfT).

Vehicles with more than 12 passenger seats, including works buses, minibuses used under a Minibus Permit and buses which may lawfully be used on a road without a CIF (ie Community Buses and LEA school buses) require a *Class V test*. This is similar to a car MOT test but must be carried out:

(a) at a DfT testing station
(b) by a designated council, or
(c) by an authorised examiner whose authorisation permits him to test vehicles in this class.

Drivers of such vehicles should check that their "authorised examiner" is permitted to test Class V vehicles. PSVs with more than eight seats and having a CIF and large buses (designed to carry more than 16 passengers, excluding the driver) require a Class VI test which is conducted by a DfT vehicle examiner either at a VOSA testing station or at certain designated premises. This test is more rigorous and comprehensive than the Class IV or V MOT tests and covers every item specified in the *PSV Inspection Manual* (available from TSO).

Summary

As previously stated, tests of passenger vehicles including PSVs and taxis are carried out anually after their first examination which is usually on or before the first anniversary of their registration (but may in a few cases be on or before their third anniversary). They may be carried out by

DfT vehicle examiners, examiners authorised by the DfT to inspect vehicles or designated councils. The table below shows, by seating capacity, the class of test to which various vehicles are subject, and by whom they are to be examined.

Class	Non PSVs	PSVs	First examination after	Examined by		
				DfT	Authorised Examiner	Designated council
IV	eight or fewer seats*	eight or fewer seats	three years		✓	✓
V	more than eight but 12 or fewer seats*		one year		✓	✓
V	more than 12 seats* including work buses and "Permit" minibuses	PSVs which can be used without CIF, i.e Community Buses, LEA's school buses	one year	✓	ø	✓
VI		PSVs with more than eight seats not in Class V	one year	✓	—	—
ø Only a few authorised examiners have the facilities to test Class V vehicles and are authorised to so so.						
* Excluding the driver's seat.						

5 FITNESS, EQUIPMENT AND USE OF PSVs AND MINIBUSES

PSV CONDITIONS OF FITNESS

The **PSV (Conditions of Fitness, Equipment, Use and Certification) Regulations 1981** (SI 1981 No. 257) are the major source of legislation covering the design of PSVs. Similar regulations apply to minibuses with between nine and 16 seats (excluding the driver's seat) used under ss.18–21 of the **Transport Act 1985** (Permit minibuses and Community Buses). These regulations place no less emphasis on safety but relax or omit many of the "comfort" requirements (eg seat spacing or headroom). Minibuses usually now comply with the criteria in Schedules 6 and 7 of the **Road Vehicle (Construction and Use) Regulations 1986** (SI 1986 No. 1078).

Many of the requirements of the regulations do not apply to vintage vehicles.

The main provisions of the **PSV (Conditions of Fitness Equipment Use and Certification) Regulations 1981** (SI 1981 No. 257) likely to be of interest to drivers are detailed below.

Stability

PSVs are "tilt tested" at their first test for a Certificate of Initial Fitness. During the test the vehicle must not overturn before the surface on which it stands has reached the following angles from the horizontal:

> Single deck fully laden Tilt angle 35°
> Double deck top deck Tilt angle 28°
> fully laden

For the test the vehicles must be loaded as shown below with weights of 63.5kg (representing a load of average passengers, driver, and, if carried, conductor).

Drivers should take great care where luggage is stowed on roof racks. It is advisable to try and prevent large numbers of school children congregating on the top deck of double deck vehicles if the lower saloon is unoccupied.

Guard rails or body "skirts" (if required due to a gap of more than 610mm between the wheels) between the front and rear wheels of a PSV must extend to within 310mm (12inches approx) of the ground, 155mm (6inches approx) from the rear wheel and 230mm (9inches approx) from the front wheel when the vehicle is unladen, with no passengers and standing on level ground.

Tilt Testing of PSVs

Single-deck vehicle — 35°

Double-deck vehicle — 28°

simulated 63.5kg passengers on upper deck, and driver (with conductor if carried)

Brakes

The EU braking regulations now apply to all passenger vehicles with eight or fewer seats, buses first used before 1 April 1983 if they have a manufacturer's Certificate of Conformity certifying that they conform to EU regulations as a "type vehicle" and buses first used after 1 April 1983.

Guard Rails

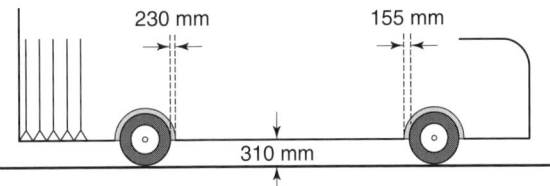

There are additional requirements for PSVs which are not "type approved".
1. All the brakes of a PSV must act directly on the wheels of the vehicle and not through the transmission. (Transmission brakes are only allowed on PSVs registered before 1 January 1955.)
2. An exception is made for mechanically operated brakes which work without the intervention of any stored energy if:
   (a) there is no universal joint between the brake and the wheel
   (b) failure of any part of the mechanism would not cause the wheel to become detached, and
   (c) all the wheels of the vehicle are fitted with brakes operated by the same means.
3. The brakes of one of the braking systems must be operated by a pedal.

Fuel Tanks

On half deck vehicles, lower decks of double deck vehicles and single deck vehicles with seats for more than 12 passengers, fuel tanks may not be positioned under gangways or within 600mm of a primary emergency exit, or anywhere in the driver or passenger compartments.

On single deck passenger vehicles carrying not more than 12 passengers the fuel tank may not be placed under or within 300mm of any entrance or exit and the filling point must not be at the rear.

Fuel tanks must only be able to be filled from outside the vehicle.

There must be a fuel cut off device accessible from outside the vehicle:
(a) on diesel engined vehicles it need not be immediately visible so long as its position is clearly marked on the outside of the vehicle and the means of operation is clearly indicated
(b) on petrol engined vehicles it must be visible and the "off" position must be marked.

(Some smaller vehicles are fitted with dashboard mounted emergency engine stops/fuel cut offs, often operated by means of the ignition key. Provided the key when turned to off stops the engine, and that the location and means of operation is correctly marked, this is not a reason for rejection when the vehicle is submitted for annual testing.)

The maintenance of fuel tanks is most important. Drivers should immediately report any insecure, leaking or corroded fuel tank or vehicles without a filler cap or with one of a type which does not prevent spillage.

Silencers and Noise

Every vehicle fitted with an internal combustion engine must be fitted with an exhaust system including a silencer. They must be maintained in good and efficient working order.

Exhaust gases must not escape into the atmosphere without first passing through the silencer fitted to the vehicle.

Vehicles are subject to spot checks on the road to ensure that they do not make more noise than the standards allow.

All vehicles registered after 1 April 1970 must meet stringent limits on noise. Newer vehicles are subject to even more stringent noise limits in so far as they relate to noise levels *measured on the road*. However, these do not apply to a vehicle proceeding to a place where by previous arrangement noise tests are to be carried out or adjustments, modifications or equipment is to be fitted so that the vehicle complies, or when a vehicle is returning from such a place immediately after the noise has been so tested.

Exhaust Pipes

Exhaust pipes must be so fitted or shielded so that there is no likelihood of any flammable material falling on them from any part of the vehicle and so that they are unlikely to cause a fire as a result of proximity to any flammable material on the vehicle.

The outlet should be either at the rear or offside and close enough to the rear to prevent, as far as possible, fumes entering the vehicle.

Drivers should report any exhaust system likely to create a fire or fume hazard, or which is wrongly positioned.

Outlets from ancillaries such as toilet, sink or cooking facilities must be designed to prevent the deposit of waste on the road surface.

Electrical Equipment

On vehicles registered on or after 19 June 1968 any electrical circuit with a voltage of over 100 volts must be capable of being isolated from the main supply by a dual pole switch readily accessible to the driver or conductor (unless one pole of the circuit is earthed).

The switch must not disconnect the obligatory lights required by the **Road Vehicles Lighting Regulations 1989**.

Body and Suspension

The body must be securely fixed to the chassis and every trap door or suspension flap secured so that it cannot become dislodged by vibration. Catches or lifting devices must not project above the floor.

The suspension must prevent any excessive body sway. Failure of any part of the suspension (except tyres) should not cause the driver to lose directional control.

On open top vehicles the side rails or panels must be at least 910mm (1.21m at the front and back) above the top deck and at least 455mm above the highest part of any seat.

Luggage Racks

These must be constructed so that any article on them, if it becomes dislodged whilst the vehicle is in motion, is unlikely to fall on the driver or affect his control.

Artificial Lighting

Adequate internal illumination must be provided on each deck of a PSV (except in the case of an open top double deck) and, on vehicles registered after 1 April 1959, on every step or platform providing an entrance or exit (other than an emergency exit).

On PSVs registered on or after 28 October 1964 there must be a dual lighting circuit so that the failure of either subcircuit does not "black out" either deck.

At least one lamp must be provided as near as is practicable to the top of every staircase leading to the top deck of a double deck vehicle.

Steps

The lowest entrance step of an unladen PSV must never be more than 435mm (approximately 17") above ground level. However, lower values are required for buses used on local and scheduled services.

Drivers should immediately report:
(a) a tread case, step, stairway or platform found to be weak or insecure, or excessively worn, or with inadequate anti-slip covering
(b) a lighting deficiency causing inadequate illumination of step, stairs, platform or interior

(c) lighting circuits not split, so that a failure of one circuit does not leave part illumination on each deck.

Entrances and Exits

Every vehicle first used after October 1987 must have a *primary* emergency exit of the height of (1.37m) leading directly from the saloon of a single deck bus or the lower deck of a double deck bus directly to the outside of the vehicle. *Secondary* emergency exits are openings of smaller dimensions. Where only two exits are specified there must be one on either side of the vehicle and there must be an emergency exit on the top deck of double deckers.

The regulations relating to the minimum number of exits depend on the vehicle's age and seating capacity.

No. of Seats	Age of Vehicle	Min No. of Exits	
		Primary	Secondary
45 or less	Pre 1981	—	2†
	Post 1981	1	1*
Over 45	Pre 1981	2	1
	Post 1981	1	2*
† one may also serve as a primary exit.			
* one must be of no smaller dimensions than a primary exit.			

In addition, double-decked coaches first used from 1 April 1990 must be fitted with a means of escape in both halves of the vehicle either by the provision of a second staircase or a hammer or other device which can be used to break any side window of the vehicle in case of an emergency. If the latter is to be used it must be displayed in a conspicuous position on the upper deck with an "IN EMERGENCY" sign together with instructions on use nearby.

Note: The main passenger entrance may also qualify as an *exit*.

Every *entrance* of a vehicle must be on the nearside but one or more entrances may be placed on the offside (not counting as legally required exits) provided they are fitted with doors controlled by the driver from his seat with a controlling device which is clearly separate and distinguishable from any device for opening or closing any entrance door on the nearside. Such doors are often referred to as "Continental Exits" intended for use in countries where vehicles are driven on the right-hand side of the road.

The minimum width of entrances is 530mm.

All *emergency exits* must be clearly *marked* both inside and on the outside if they can be opened therefrom, fitted with forward opening doors and readily accessible to passengers. Emergency exits in single deck vehicles or on the lower decks of double deck vehicles must be situated so that passengers can step directly from the gangway to the outside of the vehicle. Manually controlled emergency exit doors must always be unlocked when the vehicle is moving. Emergency exit doors on some moving vehicles can be locked with a speed-related interlock — provided that those doors can be manually opened when the vehicles are stationary. The driver must always check that the gangways are clear.

The means of operation of doors fitted to emergency exits (which must *not* be power operated) must be clearly indicated and readily accessible to persons of normal height standing outside the vehicle.

Doors

There must be a means of securing the door closed, eg a catch, on every entrance and exit.

If a door on a vehicle is capable of remaining open whilst the vehicle is in motion, or may be accidentally closed whilst the vehicle is in motion, there must also be a means of securing it open.

Each door must have two devices (eg handles) for operating it:
- (a) for normal operation which may be by the vehicle owner or person authorised by him or her, and
- (b) for operating the door from outside the vehicle.

They must be designed to operate with a single movement of the handle and the means of operation must be clearly indicated.

The direction of any manual effort required to operate must be shown (eg "pull to open") and, if the door is power operated, there must be a statement that it may only be used by passengers in an emergency.

If the door operating device is not placed on the door itself:

(a) it must be placed where it is readily associated with it and

(b) its location must be clearly indicated.

All devices must be capable of being operated by a person of normal height (without risk of being struck by the door where the device is not on the door itself) and be so designed that they cannot be accidentally dislodged.

Every door must operate without obstructing access to any entrance or exit from inside or outside the vehicle.

If a door on a vehicle is *power operated* and projects more than 80mm from the side (excluding any mouldings) when opened it must be *interlocked* with the transmission so that the vehicle cannot move off with the door open (except when operated in an emergency as above).

The operation of the brakes must be in no way adversely affected by the operation of any power operated door. If the power operated system fails, the door must be capable of being opened manually.

On vehicles having power operated doors, if the interlocking between the door operating mechanism and the transmission, referred to above, is absent, the vertical edges of the doors must be fitted with soft rubber.

All vehicles registered on or after 1 April 1980 with power operated doors fitted more than 500mm behind the back of the driver's seat must, from 1 April 1993, meet three conditions.

1. Automatically re-open if prevented from closing by an object 60mm high (eg a foot).

2. Automatically re-open if fingers or a hand are trapped, unless these can be "readily extracted".
3. Have a "tell tale" light visible to the driver to warn if not fully closed.

Drivers should report immediately if a flap or door has a broken or loose hinge, or is damaged so that it cannot be secured or held open, or has a sharp or protruding edge or defective locking mechanism.

Access to Exits

There must be unobstructed access to at least two exits from every seat in a vehicle (unless the fitness regulations require only a single exit).

This requirement need not be met in the case of:
(a) any seat beside the driver's seat, accessible by a single entrance other than the driver's door
(b) a seat on an open top of a double deck vehicle, having unobstructed access to one exit.

A barrier placed at the foot of the staircase on a double deck vehicle to prevent passengers riding upstairs (eg in "off peak" operation) does not prevent the vehicle complying with this regulation.

No seat may be fitted to any door of a PSV.

Drivers should report immediately if the access to an exit or emergency exit is obstructed (or if the means of breaking any windows designated as emergency exits are missing, inadequate or not clearly marked).

Every gangway on a PSV must be at least 305mm wide at deck level, widening further at "hip" and "shoulder" level. Passages of similar width must be provided between gangways and emergency exits and, on vehicles with seats for more than 12 passengers, gangways must be increased in width to 530mm within 910mm of any entrance or exit.

The minimum prescribed heights of gangways in vehicles adapted to carry more than 12 passengers are as follows.

Single deck vehicles and lower decks of double deck vehicles:

with 14 or fewer seats	1.6m
with more than 14 seats	1.77m
top deck of double deck vehicles	1.72m

The minimum height of gangways on vehicles with seats for 12 or fewer passengers is 1.42m reducing to 1.21m at points within 305mm of any entrance or exit.

Drivers should report a dangerously worn or contaminated gangway or entrance mat.

Seating

The supports of all seats must be securely fixed in position.

Each seat must have a closed back rest designed to prevent passengers' pockets being picked from behind.

The positioning of seats on PSVs is governed by the minimum dimensions shown.

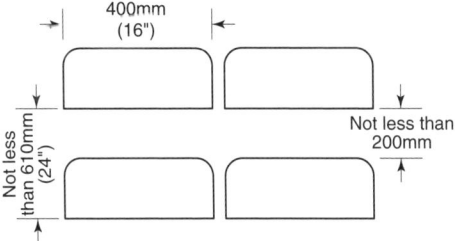

There must be protection, in the form of a guard rail or screen, for seated passengers, where there is any likelihood of their being thrown against an entrance or exit.

The front of any seat must not be any closer than 225mm to any well or step.

Drivers should report:
(a) distorted or fractured seat frames
(b) insecure seating
(c) insecure fittings or arm rests having sharp projections
(d) dirty or damaged seat coverings

(e) dirty or defective seat belts.

Courier seats

Crew seats (as the regulations describe these folding seats) may now be fitted at the front of PSVs.

The requirements for the construction and use of courier/crew seats are that they must be provided with arm rests and a suitable place for the occupant to rest his or her feet. There must be at least 300mm clear space in front of the leading edge of the crew seat and, whether in or out of use, the crew seat must not impede the driver's field of vision. When in use it is permissible for the crew seat to protrude into the gangway but those parts which do protrude must automatically retract when the seat is not in use.

The words "for crew use only" must be marked on or near each crew seat in letters at least 10mm tall.

Driver's Accommodation

The driver must have a means of preventing light from the vehicle interior disturbing him or her, and, if the vehicle has more than 12 seats, the driver's seat must be adjustable both vertically and horizontally.

Where access to this seat is from the offside, the means of entry must be at least 455mm wide and provided with a grab handle and step if the entrance is more than 690mm above the ground. If the cab is enclosed there must be an emergency escape window at least 530mm × 455mm other than on the offside.

On all vehicles with more than 12 passenger seats where access to the driver's seat is by means of a passage, the passage must be at least 300mm wide.

Ventilation

This must be adequate for driver and passengers without the need to open a window to demist the windscreen. Drivers should report missing, inoperative or blocked demisting and ventilating equipment.

Windscreens

These must be capable of being opened to give the driver a clear view ahead unless there is an adequate demisting and defrosting device. In practice the demisting requirement is normally met.

Signals

A means of signalling the driver to stop must be provided on passenger vehicles with 12 or more seats. Drivers should report any broken or missing system of passenger communication.

EQUIPMENT OF PSVs

Fire Extinguishers and First Aid

Every PSV must carry a fire extinguisher to British Standard E5423:1977, 1980 or 1987 or EN3 containing water or AFFF (foam). Every vehicle on non-local services must carry a first aid box suitable for storing the items referred to.

These must be:
(a) readily available for use
(b) clearly marked as a first aid box, or, if a fire extinguisher, with the appropriate BSI specification number
(c) maintained in good order.

The items to be carried in the first aid box, which must be of good and reliable quality and suitable design, are:
(a) 10 antiseptic wipes, foil packed
(b) one conforming disposable bandage (not less than 7.5cm wide)
(c) two triangular bandages
(d) one packet of 24 assorted adhesive dressings
(e) three large sterile unmedicated ambulance dressings (not less than 15cm × 20cm)
(f) two sterile eye pads, with attachments
(g) 12 assorted safety pins

(h) one pair of rustless blunt-ended scissors.

A first aid box which is inaccessible, obviously in poor condition, illegibly marked or missing, and a fire extinguisher which is inaccessible, obviously discharged or missing, should be immediately reported by the driver.

USE OF PSVs

Obstruction of Entrances, Exits and Gangways

No unnecessary obstruction to the above must be caused or permitted whilst passengers are being carried.

Obstruction of Driver

No person shall cause or permit any unnecessary obstruction to the driver.

Body Maintenance

Vehicles must not be used to carry passengers unless the windows, fittings and seats are in a clean and good condition.

Lamps

If carrying passengers during the hours of darkness, vehicles must have sufficient lights operating to illuminate the access to all seats and exits and any emergency exit markings. This may be extinguished on the upper deck of a double deck vehicle if a barrier is secured at the foot of all stairways.

Power Operated Doors

Except in an emergency, power operated doors may only be operated by the driver or by some other person authorised by the operator, and then not if the vehicle is in motion.

Filling of Petrol Tank

While the engine is running the petrol tank filler cap may not be removed or petrol put into the tank.

Carriage of Conductors

No vehicle with more than 20 seats may be used on a local service without a conductor unless:
  (a) it is a single deck vehicle with seats for less than 32 passengers and the emergency exit is at the front of the vehicle, visible to the driver and the entrance is also visible so that the driver is aware of any passenger trapped in the door or
  (b) it has been certified for driver-only operation under the code of practice for One Person Operation (OPO).

Carriage of Flammable or Dangerous Substances

In addition to any requirements under petroleum or similar regulations, flammable or dangerous substances may only be carried if in containers designed and constructed to minimise the risk of damage to the vehicle or injury to passengers in the event of an accident. Such containers might be used to carry a personal oxygen supply for asthmatic passengers.

Markings

The name and address of the authority, company or individual to whom the PSV "O" licence was issued and their principal place of business must be marked on the vehicle's nearside in a conspicuous position, in clearly legible characters at least 25mm tall, in colours contrasting with their background. Similarly the seating and standing capacity must be marked on the inside.

All emergency exits should be marked both inside and outside the vehicle.

Missing or illegible statutory markings should be reported by the driver.

School Bus Signs

Buses and/or coaches with nine or more passenger seats being used to transport children under the age of 16 to or from school at the start and finish of the school day must display a School Bus sign. Drivers may also use hazard warning lights when pupils are embarking or disembarking from the vehicle.

The regulations do not apply where the children are travelling on a vehicle being used to provide a registered service (so long as this is not an excursion or tour) or services which cover local registered services where 50% or more of the seats are available to the general public, or London local services (see *Local Services*).

The school bus sign does not have to be removed when children are not being carried.

6 WORKING TIME FOR DRIVERS, DRIVERS' HOURS AND RECORD KEEPING

The working time of employees in the transport industry is governed by the provisions of the Working Time Directive, originally introduced in the UK in October 1998 for workers in general and in August 2003 for road transport workers, other than drivers of vehicles that are governed by the EU Drivers' Hours regulations who are covered by the Road Transport (Working Time) Regulations introduced in the UK on 4 April 2005, and referred to under these regulations as "mobile workers". The provisions include rights for drivers to:

– work no more than an average working week of 48 hours (including overtime) averaged out over agreed reference periods
– opt out* of the 48 hours limit by agreement with his/her employer (*not available to drivers governed by the EU drivers' hours regulations)
– at least 20 days paid annual leave (including Bank and Public Holidays) which must be taken and cannot normally be exchanged for payment — see table below
– health assessments (night workers only)
– eight-hour (average) limit on night work
– daily rest of at least 11 hours
– weekly rest of at least one complete day per week or two complete days per fortnight
– breaks of at least 20 minutes after 6 continuous hours of work.

Self-employed drivers are exempt from the Working Time Regulations until 2009.

"Self-employed" means anyone who is entitled to work for him or herself, is not tied to an employer by an employment contract and who is free to organise his or her own working activities to have commercial relations with several customers.

Drivers of vehicles not subject to the EU Regulations, eg normally those driving smaller vehicles, or who work under the British Domestic Rules, continue to be covered by working time rules introduced in August 2003. The requirements for these drivers are:
- average working week of 48 hours, including overtime; individual opt-out will be available
- health assessments for night workers
- 20 days' paid leave, which, currently, can include bank and public holidays (see table below)
- adequate rest.

"Adequate rest" is defined as regular rest periods, the duration of which are expressed in units of time and which are sufficiently long and continuous to ensure that, as a result of fatigue or other irregular working patterns, workers do not cause injury to themselves, to fellow workers or to others and that they do not damage their health, either in the short term or in the longer term.

WORKING TIME RULES

This table shows application comparison of main aspects of the Road Transport Directive legislation between local bus service driver and non-regular coach service driver.

Aspect	Bus Driver	Coach Driver
Drivers' hours	"Domestic" rules (no change)	EC (Reg. 561/2006)
48-hour working week	"Opt-out" available – no limit applicable	No "opt-out" available. Max average 48-hour limit applicable
Reference period	26 weeks (up to 52 by agreement)	17/18 weeks (up to 26 weeks by agreement)
Weekly rest	"Domestic" drivers' hours rules apply	EC drivers' hours rules apply
Maximum weekly work	60 hours – increases to 78 if "opt-out" agreed	60 hours. EC drivers' hours rules apply
Night work	No limit	10 hours (longer by agreement)
Night time	Not applicable	01.00–05.00
Periods of Availability	N/A	"On-call" time and time spent travelling on a vehicle on a ferry/train and as second driver in a multi-manned vehicle.
Annual holiday	Four weeks minimum*	Four weeks minimum*
*From 1 October 2007 + 4 UK Bank/Public Holidays		
*From 1 October 2008 + 8 UK Bank/Public Holidays		
Part-time workers	Covered by "Domestic" drivers' hours rules	See "Occasional Workers"

Occasional workers	Covered by "Domestic" drivers' hours rules	Exempt from RTD limits, but EC drivers' hours rules and limits apply and must be recorded on the tachograph on each driving occasion
Records	– NOT "opted-out" — normal work/pay records to show 48-hour max. week complied with – "OPTED-OUT" — None required except the individual "opt-out" agreement itself.	– Fully required (including tachograph charts if used for "Working Time" purposes) – Plus records of all relevant ("Collective" or "Workplace") agreements – Plus time worked as a mobile worker for another employer – Must be retained for a minimum period of 2 years.

Notes to the Table

Working Time includes driving, loading and unloading, assisting passengers boarding and leaving the vehicle, cleaning and technical maintenance of the vehicle and all other work associated with the vehicle's passengers or to meet legal or regulatory obligations including completion of formalities with police, customs immigration officers, etc. Also any time during which the driver cannot freely dispose of his or her time while remaining with the vehicle — including periods of waiting not known about in advance.

Break and rest times and periods of availability are not included as working time.

Periods of availability are those periods known in advance by the driver, during which he or she is *not required to remain with the vehicle* but must remain available (on call) to start or resume work.

Occasional workers are employees who do qualifying work for fewer than:
– 11 days during a reference period of up to 26 weeks, or
– 16 days during a reference period of 26 or more weeks.

Records of work — where tachographs are used to produce records of work for working time purposes, the modes for "On Duty" and "Other Work" must be used with care for separate purposes. The "On Duty" switch is to be used to record periods of availability known about in advance, whereas the "Other Work" switch is to be used for periods of waiting not known about in advance.

Drivers' hours are strictly controlled by legislation and European Community (EC) law prevails for the majority of commercial operations. Where vehicles, or the type of work being carried out, are exempt from EC law, British regulations, in the form of the **Transport Act 1968** as modified, apply in Great Britain. If journeys are made to countries outside the European Community, either the domestic laws of the country concerned must be adhered to, or if the country is a party to the European agreement on international road transport (AETR) those rules must be followed although in the latter case they are currently (at the time of writing) aligned with the EC Regulation 3820/85.

Drivers' hours regulations can be briefly summarised as follows.

1. EC Regulation 561/2006 applies to drivers operating passenger vehicles with 9 or more passenger seats engaged on *Community regulated journeys or work* both within the United Kingdom (known as national journeys) or, when travelling to or from other Member States of the European Community (known as international journeys).

2. AETR rules (which are aligned with EC rules) apply to drivers operating passenger vehicles with nine or more

passenger seats to countries which are outside the EC but are a party to the AETR agreement, ie the CIS, Andorra, Iceland, Lichtenstein, Norway, Turkey and the former Yugoslavian countries.
3. British domestic legislation applies to drivers who drive certain vehicles or perform certain types of work exempt from the EC rules. Some exemptions apply generally whilst others apply only to journeys within Great Britain. Passenger vehicles with 12 or fewer seats (excluding the driver's seat) are exempt from this legislation if the vehicle is not used for hire or reward operations, ie private use.
4. Mixed driving is where a driver changes from driving under EC rules to driving under British rules and vice-versa.

In the following pages each set of rules is given in detail.

Drivers of vehicles used by the armed forces, police and fire brigades are exempt from the regulations.

A driver is anyone who drives a vehicle, either regularly or occasionally, even for a short period, or is carried on the vehicle in order to be available for driving if necessary, including part time drivers such as maintenance staff and technicians or employees who have to use a vehicle as a means of transporting themselves in the course of the owner's business.

Persons driving vehicles to which the British domestic hours rules (in the form of the **Transport Act 1968**) either as employees or, self employed, are also drivers.

OFFENCES

It is an offence to contravene any part of the drivers' hours regulations and heavy fines can be imposed on a driver (up to £5000) if convicted. The employer may also be prosecuted and in very severe cases both the driver and the employer can face a prison sentence — in these circumstances the operator's licence may also be put at risk.

It is, therefore, very important for a driver to fully understand the rules governing his working hours so that infringements are avoided.

Prohibition of Certain Types of Payment

Under EC law it is an offence for payments in the form of bonuses, etc to be made for distance travelled if this is likely to endanger road safety.

"COMMUNITY REGULATED" JOURNEYS

EC Regulation 561/2006 applies to drivers of passenger vehicles with seats for nine or more passengers (excluding the driver's seat) unless the vehicle or the operation is exempt. A list of the exemptions is given below but the most useful exemption applies to passenger vehicles on regular services, where the route covered by the service does not exceed 50km. A return journey over the same route is not included when determining route length. Therefore, Community regulations apply to a vehicle if it has nine or more passenger seats and it is used on either:

(a) a regular service over 50km. This could include some regular contracts such as schools and works journeys, if over this distance and longer distance regular services whether "express" or "stopping", or

(b) "occasional" and "shuttle" services. In practice these EC terms cover private hire work and excursions and tours — unless the latter have been registered as local services because they operate one or more times per week over at least six consecutive weeks.

In conjunction with the above-mentioned regulation, EC Regulation 3821/85 also applies and this is concerned with the type of record of their working hours that drivers must keep, namely the tachograph chart. Details of these regulations will be found under *The Tachograph*.

Daily Driving Period

This is a maximum of *nine hours* which may be extended to *10 hours* maximum not more than twice a week.

The daily driving period is defined as being the period at work between any two daily rest periods or between a daily and a weekly rest period.

Total Fortnightly Driving

Total fortnightly driving is *90 hours* maximum.

Note: A driver can drive up to a total of *56 hours* in one week but is restricted to *34 hours* in the second so that over the two consecutive weeks the limit is not exceeded.

Driving Time

A driver may drive for not more than a total of 4½ hours (which can be either continuous or accumulated) without taking a qualifying break or breaks.

Breaks from Driving

After not more than a total of 4½ hours' continuous driving a break of at least *45 minutes* must be taken unless the driver begins a rest period. Alternatively, where driving is not continuous, the 45 minutes can be split into two shorter periods — one of which must be 15 minutes (minimum) and be followed by one of at least 30 minutes (which must be taken before driving is resumed) so that they aggregate 45 minutes spread within the combined working period or including the 30 minutes (minimum) immediately following it. When 45 minutes break has been taken, either as a single break or an aggregate of two separate shorter periods, the calculation of driving time must start afresh taking no account of previous driving periods and breaks (*R v Charlton et al* 1993).

During a break the driver must use the time exclusively for recuperation and must not carry out any other work. However, subject to case law, waiting time and time spent in the passenger seat of a vehicle in motion, on a ferry or a train, might be regarded as such other work.

Daily Rest Period

In each 24-hour period counting from the start of work, a driver must have a daily rest of at least *11 consecutive hours* which may be reduced without compensation to not less than *nine consecutive hours* on three occasions between weekly rest periods. However, on days when the daily rest period is not reduced a driver is allowed to take a minimum of 12 hours of rest split into two separate periods during the 24 hours, the first being a minimum of three hours and the last period of which must be of at least *nine consecutive hours*.

Double ("Multi") Manning

Where a vehicle is manned by at least two drivers, each driver must have a rest period of not less than *nine consecutive hours* during each continuous period of 30 hours (making the maximum permitted length of their working day = 21 hours before rest commences).

In order for a relief driver to benefit from the Community drivers' hours relaxation for double manning he or she must work/travel in a vehicle with a co-driver(s) at all times for the first hour of double/multi manning, where the presence of another driver in the vehicle is optional.

Note: Where journeys involve the use of ferries or trains, drivers may interrupt an 11-hour daily rest period, not more than twice, provided that the breaks combined do not exceed one hour and the driver(s) has access to a bunk or couchette during all parts of the rest period.

Drivers may choose not to take time spent on board a ferry or train as part of the daily rest period; such time would then be regarded as a break — see under *Breaks from Driving*

Weekly Rest Period

During each week a daily rest period must be extended into a weekly rest period totalling *45 consecutive hours*, however on alternate weeks, this rest may be reduced to *24 consecutive hours*. Each such reduced rest period must be made good by the driver taking an equivalent rest period *en bloc* before the end of the *third week* following the week in question.

A weekly rest period beginning in one week and continuing into the next can be attached to either week.

Any compensatory rest period taken for a reduced weekly rest period must be attached to another rest period of at least *nine hours*.

The definition of a "week" is the period between 00.00 hours Monday and 24.00 hours Sunday.

Daily and reduced weekly rest periods taken away from the driver's base may be taken in the vehicle at the discretion of the driver, provided the vehicle is fitted with suitable sleeping facilities for each driver and the vehicle is *stationary*.

Maximum Number of Consecutive Daily Driving Periods

A driver must, after no more than six consecutive daily driving periods, take a weekly rest period.

However, provided he or she has not exceeded the maximum permitted weekly driving hours, he or she may postpone his or her weekly rest period until the end of the sixth 24-hour rest period (from the end of the previous weekly rest period). He or she may continue to drive during this period of postponement up to his or her maximum permitted weekly driving hours of 56 hours.

Emergencies

Article 12 of the regulations allows a driver, provided that road safety is not jeopardised, to depart from the driving restrictions to enable him to reach a suitable stopping place to ensure the safety of persons and of the vehicle. In these circumstances the reason must be recorded on the tachograph chart or print-out. (For details of the tachograph regulations see *The Tachograph*.)

Periodic Checks

Article 10 requires an employer and associated undertakings (eg tour operators and driver employment agencies) to organise work in such a way that drivers do not infringe either the hours or the tachograph rules. It further requires employers to make periodic checks to ensure that the regulations have been complied with. If breaches are found steps must be taken to prevent their repetition.

Employers will be liable for infringements committed by their drivers in any EC Member State or where these EC rules apply.

EXEMPTIONS FROM EU RULES

See *British Domestic Operations*.

Certain vehicles and/or their use are exempted from EU Regulation 561/2006 and these exemptions and supplementary provisions are fully defined for the UK in The Community Drivers' Hours and Recording Equipment Regulations 2007 (SI 2007 No. 1819).

The following are exempt.

1. Minibuses and vehicles with between 10 and 17 seats including the driver's seat, used exclusively for the non-commercial carriage of passengers. (DfT guidance on the meaning of exclusively non-commercial currently excludes minibuses used as part of a commercial operation to move staff — even if its passengers did not pay a fare of any kind.)
2. Vehicles of any size when used on regular services where the single route length does not exceed 50km.

    A regular service is one that carries passengers:
    (a) at specified intervals
    (b) along specified routes

(c) using pre-determined stopping places.

It should not be assumed that all local services fall within British domestic rules. The 50km route length refers to a single journey length measuring the actual route taken. It is possible for a local service to exceed 50km and therefore it would be subject to EU rules on hours and records. Where a through service exceeds 50km it will be subject to EU rules and not domestic rules.

It would appear that any service which has its own identity, eg route number, service description, will come under EU rules if it exceeds 50km route length even if registered as separate components. In short, a timetabled bus or coach service that falls within the 50km measurement will be subject to British domestic rules. Also included are what are known as "Special Regular" services provided for the exclusive use of workers, schoolchildren and forces personnel. This may include, for example, regular contracts for schools and works so long as they fall within the overall meaning of "Special Regular" and are contained within the 50km limit.

3. Vehicles of any size operating exclusively on islands not exceeding 2300km^2 in area and which are not linked to the mainland by bridge, ford or tunnel. (This includes the Isles of Wight, Arran and Bute.)

4. Vehicles used for driving instruction or examination with a view to obtaining a driving licence or certificate of professional competence, provided that the vehicle is not being used for the commercial carriage of passengers or goods.

   Note: Vehicles used for route familiarisation by full PCV driving licence holders are *not* given exemption from EU rules.

5. Vehicles undergoing road tests for the purpose of technical development, repair and maintenance, specialised breakdown vehicles, and vehicles used in emergency and rescue operations.

Other types of operation and vehicles excepted or exempted from Regulation (EC) 561/2006 include:
  (a) vehicles with a maximum authorised speed not exceeding 40kph
  (b) vehicles owned or hired without a driver by the armed forces, civil defence services, fire services, and forces responsible for maintaining public order when the carriage is undertaken as a consequence of the tasks assigned to these services and is under their control
  (c) any vehicle which is propelled by steam or was manufactured before 1947 and commercial vehicles which have historic status according to the legislation of the Member State in which they are being driven and which by virtue of their construction and equipment are suitable to be used for the non-commercial carriage of passengers; historic status in UK is defined as having been manufactured more than 25 years before the date on which the vehicle is being driven
  (d) specially fitted mobile project vehicles, the primary purpose of which is use as an educational facility when stationary
  (e) vehicles used exclusively on roads inside hub facilities such as ports, interports and railway terminals.

"Dead" or "Out of Service" Journeys

An operating schedule will include not only the journeys on which passengers are carried, but also "dead" trips where the vehicle is not carrying passengers. These may be positioning trips to and from an operating base and the starting and finishing place of a passenger journey. They may also be link trips contained within a schedule to enable a vehicle to move from the end of a passenger journey at one point to the start of a passenger journey at another point.

These "dead" trips over any distance are subject to the rules applying to the passenger carrying journey to which the trip is attached.

For example, if a vehicle is required to travel empty a distance of say, five miles, for the commencement of a private hire that is subject to EU rules, then the positioning trip itself is subject to EU rules.

In like manner, a positioning trip before a local bus service (regular or special service less than 50km in length) that is subject to British domestic rules is itself subject to British domestic rules, just as are any link trips over any distance that are contained within the overall schedule of vehicle movements.

Summary of EU Drivers' Hours Regulations for PSVs

	Max / Min	Basic Rule	Relaxation
On driving without a break	Max	4h 30mins	
On breaks between driving	Min	45mins	One period of at least 15 minutes followed by one other period of at least 30 minutes
On daily driving time	Max	9h	2×10 hours in fixed week[1]
On length of working day	Max	24 − 11 = 13h*	24 − 9 = 15h*
On length of working day if double manned	Max	21h	—
On daily rest	Min	11h	3×9h between weekly rest periods

	Max / Min	Basic Rule	Relaxation
Split daily rest	Min	12h total	One rest of at least 3 hours followed by one of at least 9 hours
On daily rest if double manned	Min	9h/30h	—
On driving time between weekly rests	Max	56h	—
On fortnightly driving time	Max	90h	—
On weekly rest[2]	Min	45h after six consecutive days' work	24h minimum. Compensate "en block" before the end of the following third week.

Key

[1]Fixed week commences at midnight Sunday/Monday.

[2] The relaxation to less than 45 hours can only be taken every other week to ensure that in every two consecutive weeks the driver will have at least one weekly rest of 45 hours after a maximum of 6 days of working and at least one weekly rest of at least 24 hours after a maximum of 6 other days of working.

*Can be inferred from other limits.

DRIVERS' HOURS OF WORK RECORDS

The Tachograph

Drivers who are subject to EC Regulation 561/2006 must observe the requirements of EC Regulation 3821/85 (also applicable to AETR related journeys) which concerns the recording of a driver's working hours by means of the tachograph.

However (until 30 December 2007) as an alternative to the analogue tachograph, drivers of vehicles not fitted with a tachograph on national regular services may carry a timetable and duty roster (see below).

Since drivers on regular services not exceeding 50km route length continue to be exempt from EU drivers' hours and the need to use a tachograph, this alternative method of recording is in effect only applied to drivers on regular services over 50km route length.

The alternative is also available (until 30 December 2007) to drivers on regular international services which are cross-border services which start and finish not more than 50km "as the crow flies" from each border and where the route length, by road, does not exceed 100km.

The tachograph is an instrument (see *illustrations below*) which automatically records, by means of a chart positioned behind the clock face (or on a "smart card" — see *The Digital Tachograph*):

(a) the distance travelled by the vehicle
(b) the vehicle's speed
(c) the driving time
(d) the periods of work of the driver
(e) breaks in the working day and daily rest period and
(f) the opening of the case containing the record chart (analogue type tachograph only).

The analogue type is so constructed that the driver is able to observe that the instrument is recording properly; that the last nine hours on the chart are visible to an examiner without the need to take any action other than opening the tachograph; and (in the case of a 2-driver tachograph) that when a second driver is carried on the vehicle his or her attendance is recorded on a separate chart.

On top of the instrument is the driver mode control selector with the symbols:

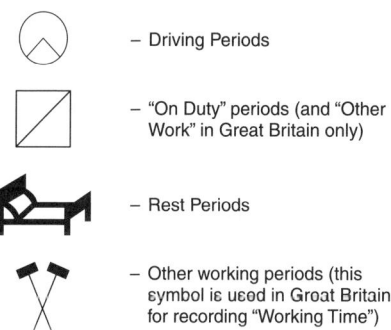

Mode Selection

When performing any function covered by the above symbols the mode selector must be set against the correct symbol otherwise the recording on the chart will be incorrect. This is an offence which could lead to prosecution.

As an example, if, during a working day averaging nine hours, the mode selector on a manual tachograph is set on the steering wheel symbol and is not changed, the record will show no breaks having been taken, the chart will only record that during the day the vehicle was stationary for a certain period of time. Since it is a requirement of the law that a break in driving must be taken, there would be no indication from the recorded details that such breaks had been observed and this would suggest an infringement of the drivers' hours rules, which might leave the driver open to prosecution.

It is, therefore, most important that the instrument is used correctly.

Two Driver Tachograph (Analogue Type)

Front View

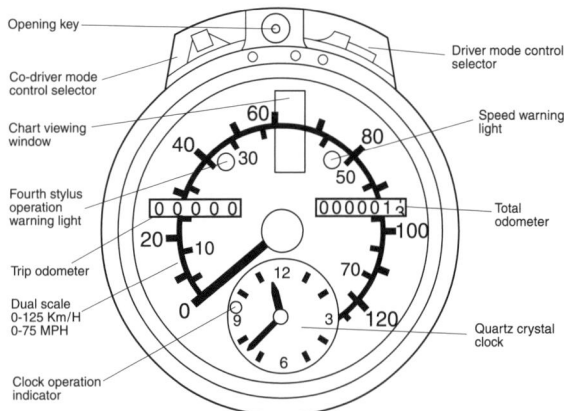

Note: The tachograph described above is the analogue/ electric tachograph which relies on pulse signals from the drive train fitted to the respective vehicle to move a needle in the unit which creates a trace on a paper disc/chart which is inserted by the driver. This type of tachograph is to be gradually phased out of operation to be replaced by a digital version which stores information on microchip and "smartcards". It will be sufficiently "intelligent" to warn the driver when contraventions of the drivers' hours regulations are about to take place (see *The Digital Tachograph*).

Instrument checks

The instrument must be *checked* every two years and *recalibrated* every six. Plaques are attached to it showing the date when the inspections were last carried out. The two yearly checks are due either two years after the date shown on the installation plaque or two years after the date shown on the two yearly plaque, whichever is the later.

The six yearly recalibration is due six years after the date shown on the *installation* plaque regardless of any two yearly inspections.

At the time of recalibration all existing plaques are removed, new plaques are fitted and the next inspection is then due two years later.

In some cases the two and six yearly inspections may never be reached, because if the instrument develops a fault it must be examined and repaired or replaced at a tachograph centre. When this happens a new plaque is attached to it which means that the time limits start again.

The two yearly plaque appears below.

```
TWO YEARLY INSPECTION
Centre/Seal No .......................
Date ...................................
```

The six yearly recalibration plaque is similar to the illustration below.

```
Date      ...................................
'l' ......................................mm
'w' ......................................
rev/km
                                   imp/km
Seal No ...................................
```

Failure to comply with these requirements can incur a fine on summary conviction.

Example of a Used Tachograph Chart

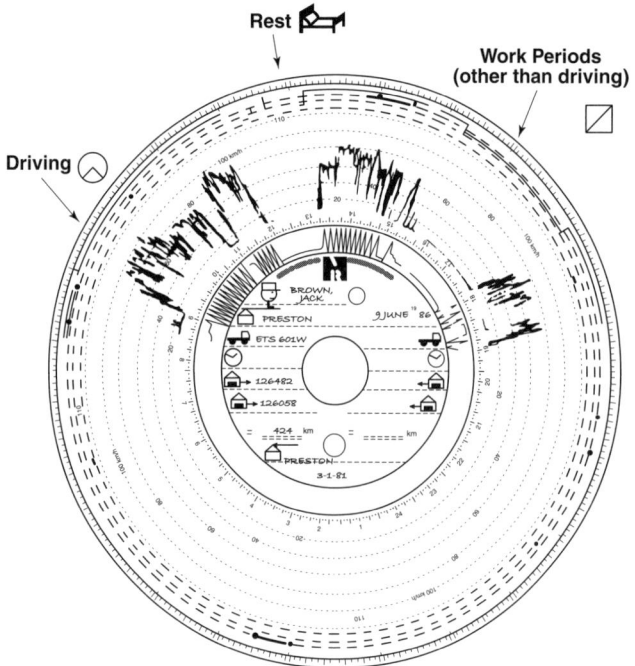

The chart

The chart (see *Example of a Used Tachograph Chart*) is a specially wax-coated disc which comprises a centre field for recording certain particulars by hand. Radiating outwards are various concentric rings — the first being a distance (km) trace, followed by the various activity symbols and finally the speed symbol. On the outer edge are the time segments up to 24 hours.

Note: There are variations in the make-up of different types of charts, depending on the make of instrument used, but the basic information remains the same. Employers must issue charts (paper rolls for the digital tachograph) which are compatible with the tachographs fitted in the vehicles to be driven by the employee.

The distance, activity and speed traces are all marked automatically by the various styli fitted in the instrument and it is apparent from this that the mode selector referred to earlier must always be correctly positioned for the activity being carried out.

Care must be taken in handling charts as they can scratch and become damaged quite easily. By law damaged or dirty charts must not be used.

The chart must always face upwards when placed in the instrument.

Note: In some tachographs it is necessary to have a blind chart inserted when the vehicle is not in use to protect the styli from being damaged; this is because the mechanism continues to revolve whilst the clock is operating.

The instrument also has a speed warning light which allows a maximum operational speed to be set by the operator and if the limit is exceeded the warning light is illuminated. Drivers should be advised by their employers if operational maximum speeds are set.

Drivers' responsibilities

It is the driver's responsibility to complete the charts correctly and this means that from the moment of taking over the vehicle the driver must use a chart to record his or her driving and working time, etc. Before inserting the chart in the tachograph, the following particulars must be manually entered in the centre field on the front face of the chart:

(a) surname and first name
(b) the date and place of commencement of chart
(c) the registration number of the vehicle
(d) the odometer reading at the start of the first journey.

At the end of the working period the centre field must again be completed by recording:

(a) the final odometer reading
(b) the place of finishing
(c) the date.

Travelling to and from a vehicle under the employer's instructions must be recorded manually as duty time. (Skills Motor Coaches et al, 2001.)

If, during a working period, a change of vehicle takes place, this must be manually recorded on the chart (there is usually space on it to record at least two changes) and particulars of the new vehicle, together with the time of change, noted. If the second vehicle has a different make of tachograph, a different type of chart might be required. Only a chart compatible with that instrument must be used and the same procedure applied. At the end of the day all charts used must be kept together so that a complete record is available.

Whilst in charge of the vehicle the driver is responsible for seeing that the instrument is working correctly and that the mode is set properly for recording the various activities.

The time recorded on the chart must at all times agree with the current official time in the country of registration of the vehicle. (If a GB registered vehicle is on an international journey the clock should remain set at the official time in Great Britain and not changed on entering different time zones abroad.) The driver must also check that the time of day is correct when placing the chart in the instrument.

Currently while on duty the driver must have in his or her possession the completed current week's charts and the charts for the previous 15 days for possible inspection by the enforcement authorities. Currently, completed charts must be returned to the employer within 21 days but drivers may request copies for their own personal use from their employer. Failure to return charts within the time limit is an offence and carries a heavy fine on summary conviction. These requirements change on 1 January 2008 when drivers must retain in their possession the charts for the current day and the previous 28 days. Accordingly, drivers must return completed charts to their employer within 35 days from the date of use.

An authorised examiner can enter the vehicle and inspect the instrument and inspect and copy or, if he suspects them of being false or having been tampered with, remove and retain any charts found therein. If a chart is retained by an authorised examiner or police officer for checking, a receipt should be issued to the driver showing the date and time of the occurrence. If a new chart has to be fitted the official should be asked to note the circumstances on that chart for record and future inspection purposes.

If the tachograph develops a fault or ceases to function, manual records must continue to be made of the various activities, either on the chart, on a temporary chart or a sheet of paper. Whatever method is used the original chart plus any temporary chart or sheet of paper must be kept together so that a complete record of the working period is available. On returning to the depot the driver must notify the employer so that arrangements can be made for repairs to be carried out at an approved centre. It is a legal requirement that the instrument be repaired as soon as circumstances permit. However, if the vehicle is unlikely to return to the depot within a period of one week calculated from the day of the breakdown or discovery of defective operation, the employer must arrange for the repair to be carried out en route.

When the tachograph was originally installed it would have been calibrated and sealed — there can be at least six seals attached to it — and these seals must not be tampered with. If the seals are broken for any reason the circumstances must be noted by the driver and the employer informed so that new seals can be attached by a tachograph centre (see also *Instrument Checks* above).

Repairs, recalibration and sealing can only take place at an approved tachograph centre. If for any reason there is a delay in having the instrument attended to, the driver should carry in the cab either a note or some other proof that the vehicle has been booked in for repair on a certain date. This should satisfy an examiner if the driver is stopped during a period when manual records are being kept because of the state of the instrument.

If a chart is damaged during a working day it must not be thrown away but kept and at the end of the working period attached to the replacement chart when taken from the tachograph.

Two or more employers

If a driver works for more than one employer each employer must be notified of the name and address of the other(s) and completed charts must be returned by the driver to the first employer irrespective of who supplied the charts.

Failure to notify each employer of the circumstances is an offence and can incur a heavy fine on summary conviction.

Employers' responsibilities

Under the new EU Drivers' Hours regulations, the employer is responsible for any relevant offences resulting from the actions of his or her employees.

It is the employer's responsibility to issue sufficient charts and paper rolls of the right type for the operation involved, bearing in mind the possibility of charts being damaged or removed by law enforcement officers. It is therefore a good idea for the driver to have at least seven days' supply.

The employer must ensure that completed charts are returned by drivers as soon as reasonably practical and the charts must be kept in good order for at least 12 months and be made available for inspection by law enforcement officers if required.

All these requirements apply equally to the owner-driver. Employers must give copies of record sheets to employees who ask for them.

From 1 January 2008, drivers must return completed charts to their employers within 35 days from the date of use.

Records (charts) used in evidence
The traces on the chart produced by the tachograph and any manual entries made on the chart may be evidence, and in Scotland sufficient evidence, of the matters appearing from them as they affect drivers' hours and record keeping. Other traces which also show on the chart, eg a vehicle exceeding the speed limit, will not normally be accepted as evidence unless it is corroborated by other evidence such as a police patrol, radar, or camera check.

Offences
Apart from the offences already mentioned, it is an offence:
   (a) if the vehicle to which the regulations apply does not have a tachograph or
   (b) if the instrument is installed and is not being used in accordance with the regulations, eg tampering with the instrument to produce false records, etc.

Heavy fines can be imposed on summary conviction. It is a defence when it is proved that:
   (a) the vehicle was proceeding to a tachograph centre for the equipment to be installed
   (b) the equipment was not working correctly because it could not be repaired by an approved fitter or workshop
   (c) manual recordings were being made by drivers whilst the equipment was inoperable.

Similarly, where seals are broken or removed, it is not an offence if:
   (a) the action was unavoidable
   (b) it was not possible for the seals to be replaced by an approved fitter or workshop
   (c) the equipment in all other respects was being used in accordance with the regulations.

Reminders
The centre field of the chart must be completed *before* placing it in the instrument and again when finishing the working day or when a change of vehicle takes place.

If working away from the vehicle for any length of time the driver should make sure that the mode selector is correctly positioned for recording the working time; alternatively, the chart should be removed and details entered by hand on the reverse side of the chart (this is especially important if the vehicle is left standing for any period, ie in the yard where someone else could drive it). The driver may also be taking a statutory break during this period, which must be recorded.

Note: Manual entries can be made anywhere on a chart as long as the chart remains undefaced. Manual entries on the reverse of the chart are the safest and some charts provide dedicated spaces for such entries.

Drivers should remember to operate the mode selector switch so that it is recording the work actually being performed at any given time (see *Mode Selection*).

The EU regulations provide that where the driver is away from the vehicle and unable to operate the equipment in person, the various records of time must (either manually or by automatic recording or otherwise) be legibly entered on the sheet without damaging it. *Thus there is no legal requirement to leave charts in tachographs overnight but if operating on a journey outside the United Kingdom it is advisable to leave the chart in the instrument until replaced by a new chart (but not longer than 24 hours). Enforcement authorities in some other EC countries will not accept manual entries on the chart face other than those required in the centre field.*

The chart can be left in the instrument for up to 24 hours but it is advisable only to do this if it is certain that the vehicle will not be moved during the driver's absence and that the driver will return before the chart overruns.

Drivers should note that the chart is a personal record of the hours they have worked; it is not a log for the vehicle.

Daily continuity of charts assists enforcement staff. Where continuity is broken, a manual entry giving the reason for the break, eg "Commencing weekly rest" or "Commencing sick leave", on the last chart before the break, is useful to assist enforcement officers, drivers and employers should any need arise for any investigation of the records.

Service Timetable and Duty Roster

Until 30 December 2007, drivers on regular services within the United Kingdom may, on vehicles not fitted with a tachograph, carry with them a timetable and duty roster. A regular service is a service operating at specified intervals along specified routes calling at predetermined stops.

Operators must construct a service timetable and duty roster and a copy of that part relating to the driver's own route must be carried on the vehicle.

The service timetable must show the pattern of the service in sufficient detail to indicate that it is being followed and the driver must carry a copy whilst at work.

The duty roster must show each driver's name, date of birth, base and duty schedule for the current week, the preceding week and the following week (three weeks in all). The schedule must show the driver's daily rest periods, breaks, driving periods, and other periods of duty. It must be signed by the service operator and the driver must carry his or her own personal extract whilst at work. It must be kept by the operator for one year after the expiry of the period covered. Drivers must be given extracts from it if they so request.

Exemptions
A driver does not have to keep records if driving a passenger vehicle with nine or fewer seats including the driver's seat, or a passenger vehicle on a "regular service" of not more than 50km in route length.

Note: Whilst record keeping is not required in these circumstances, operators have the right to ask drivers to keep some form of record and are themselves advised to keep detailed supporting records of their drivers' work, since compliance with the rules relating to hours of work involves both retrospective checks and careful scheduling.

THE DIGITAL TACHOGRAPH

This type of tachograph uses computer and "smart card" technology to record information similar to that recorded on the paper chart by the analogue type of tachograph. The digital information is recorded on an internal memory and on a magnetic strip on a credit card-sized Driver's Card. Digital tachographs will gradually replace the analogue type as only the digital type can be fitted to vehicles first registered after 1 May 2006.

The digital tachograph is an instrument that automatically records:
  (a) distance travelled by the vehicle
  (b) speed of the vehicle (in detail for the last 24 hours and any periods of more than one minute where the speed limiter set speed has been exceeded)
  (c) driving time (daily and weekly)
  (d) periods of work of drivers (daily and weekly)
  (e) breaks and rest periods (daily and weekly).

Information Storage/Access

Print-outs
The information stored in the tachograph can be printed out onto a paper roll. The employer is responsible for supplying the driver with the correct type of roll and for retaining print-outs as records in the same manner as the paper charts used in analogue tachographs. Spare rolls must be carried on the vehicle to enable VOSA and police officers to take a print-out when enforcement checks are carried out.

Drivers are entitled to print-outs on request to the employer.

DIGITAL TACHOGRAPH

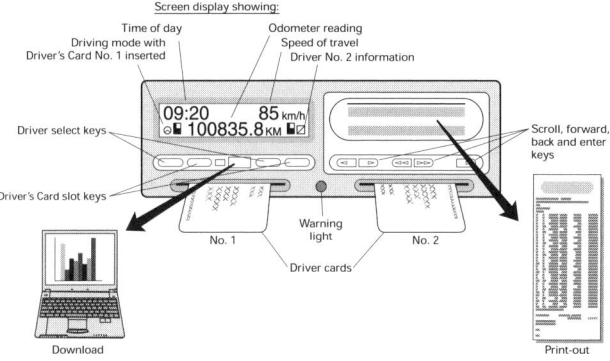

Driver's card

This card (white) holds 28 driving days' worth of time, distance and activity data but does not hold vehicle speed data. The card is personal to the driver concerned and must always be available when the driver is at work. The card is valid for five years.

Note: 1. Where a driver card is damaged, malfunctions or is not in the possession of the driver, the driver must:
    (a) at the start of a journey, print out the details of the vehicle he or she is driving and manually endorse that print-out with his or her name, driver card or driver licence number, all other periods of work and availability together with details of any breaks in work and daily rest periods
    (0) at the end of driving, print out the information relating to periods of time recorded by the tachograph, record any periods of other work, availability and rest undertaken since the print-out that was made at the start of driving, and mark on the second print-out his or her driver identity details and signature.

2. When, as a result of being away from the vehicle, the driver is unable to use the tachograph, he or she must manually enter onto the driver card details of periods of work and availability and any breaks in work and any daily rest periods using the manual entry facility provided on the tachograph.

Company card
This card (yellow) enables access to data stored in the tachograph which relates to the company and the driver. It is valid for five years.

Workshop card
This card (red) is used by VOSA approved/authorised technicians at approved testing centres to enable unlimited access to the data stored in the tachograph. The card is personal to the technician concerned and is valid for one year only.

Control card
This card (blue) is only issued to and used by the enforcement authorities. It permits unlimited access to all the data stored in the tachograph (and on the driver's card when that is inserted). It is valid for two years only.

Downloading of Data
Data held within the tachograph may be downloaded (transferred) to a computer for analysis and storage by the operator of the vehicle. Any such downloaded material must be made available for VOSA, etc enforcement checks and any information downloaded from the driver card must be copied to the driver on request.

Enforcement Checks

Authorised officials throughout the EU can check a vehicle at any time for drivers' hours/records compliance purposes. In the case of vehicles fitted with a digital tachograph, such checks may now cover the activities of the driver in a different Member State of the EU than the one in which the check is taking place and can also cover the activities of previous drivers on that vehicle.

Thus, a driver and the operator can be fined in one state for offences (including previous drivers' offences) which took place in another state. Fines may be fixed penalties and points may be awarded UK driving licences.

FEES FOR CARDS

The regulations also provide for fees to be charged in respect of driver cards and operator (company) cards. Fees will not be payable in respect of workshop cards, or control cards which may be held by police officers and VOSA officers.

First issue card	£38
Renewal of time expired card	£19
Replacement for damaged, lost or stolen card	£19

In Great Britain, the cards will be issued by the Driver and Vehicle Licensing Agency (DVLA).

AETR

The European Agreement concerning the work of crews of vehicles engaged in international road transport, AETR, is not an EC agreement but embodies a larger group of European countries which includes the United Kingdom and other EC Member States (see *Drivers' Hours and Record Keeping*).

BRITISH DOMESTIC OPERATIONS

Domestic legislation in the form of the **Transport Act 1968** Part VI, as modified, applies within Great Britain to drivers of vehicles which are exempt from EC law. (See *"Community Regulated" Journeys*)

Domestic Hours Limits

The provisions of the **Transport Act 1968** apply. However these were relaxed in 1971 by the **Drivers' Hours (Passenger and Goods Vehicles) (Modifications) Order 1971** to exclude any limits on the amounts of daily and weekly duty apart from a prescribed maximum length of working day.

Driving Time

Driving is defined as time spent at the controls of the vehicle for the purpose of controlling its movement whether it is in motion or stationary with the engine running. If some driving is done off the road, eg within the private grounds of an educational establishment, this does not count as driving time but as part of the duty time.

Maximum Total Daily Driving Time

No driver may drive a vehicle for an aggregate time in excess of 10 hours per working day.

Continuous Driving Without a Break

A driver must take a break of at least *30 minutes* after driving continuously (ie without the driving being broken by breaks satisfying the minimum length requirements) for *5½ hours*. Any other interruptions from driving (not including any shorter breaks which are intended to be aggregated to 45 minutes as below) for non-driving work can be completely ignored for the purposes of calculating the continuous driving limits, based on the cumulative aggregate of actual periods of driving.

The **Drivers' Hours (Passenger and Goods Vehicles) (Modifications) Order 1971** (SI 1971 No. 818) provides an important alternative to the 5½ hours' rule based on continuous driving. Under this Order, a driver may drive for up to 8½ hours straight through provided that within that period he or she takes breaks of non-driving time, eg layover at terminals, etc amounting in aggregate to at least 45 minutes and that the last of the driving periods marks either the end of the working day or the start of a minimum 30 minute break.

Thus, this provision means that the 8½ hour "duty" need not be the only work on that day.

Maximum Daily Duty/Spreadover

The maximum daily duty (working day) for drivers performing domestic journeys and work is precisely prescribed by the **Drivers' Hours (Passenger and Goods Vehicles) (Modifications) Order 1971** (SI 1971 No. 818) which provides for a maximum spreadover each working day of *16 hours*, which, apart from statutory break periods, may include up to *10 hours'* driving and the remainder as work other than driving.

Daily Intervals of Rest

A driver must have a period of rest under the 1971 Modifications Order of at least *10 hours* between each working day. This can be reduced on three days in the working week to 8½ hours.

Note: A working day is not a calendar day. It is a period of driving and duty separated by two statutory periods for rest. (It is of course impossible to legislate for a period of rest since the driver is free to take rest or otherwise.)

Minimum Weekly Rest

The 1971 Modifications Order provides for a rest day of *24 hours every two weeks*, ie each fortnight. The rest period does not have to be a calendar day. It can be taken at the beginning or end of a working fortnight and can fall partly in one fortnight and partly in the next, provided it is started in the fortnight to which it applies.

The definition of a "week" is the period between 00.00 hours Monday and 24.00 hours Sunday.

Emergencies

Where events cause, or are likely to cause danger to life or health of persons or animals, serious interruption in the maintenance of public services for the supply of water, gas, electricity or drainage or of telecommunication or postal services, or a serious interruption in the use of roads, railways, ports or airports, driving and duty limits may be exceeded provided the driver does not spend time on duty (other than to deal with the emergency) for periods aggregating more than 11 hours.

PSV Drivers' Hours — Domestic

	Max/Min	Basic Rule	Relaxation
On driving without a break	Max	5h 30mins	8h 30mins incorporating at least 45min aggregate breaks
On breaks	Min	30mins	45min aggregate break in 8h 30mins and followed by at least 30mins if this not end of working day
On driving time	Max	10h	—
On length of working day	Max	16h	—
On rest	Min	10h	3 × 8h 30mins in fixed week
On rest	Min	24h each 2 fixed weeks	—

MIXED DRIVING

This concerns drivers who change from community regulated operations to British domestic operations or vice versa within a working day or week. In instances where this occurs the driver has the choice of observing the EU rules all the time, or a combination of both provided the EU limits are not exceeded when engaged on EU work. The following points must also be considered.

1. Time spent driving under EU rules counts as "driving" under both sets of rules.
2. Time spent operating under domestic rules counts as "other work" under Community rules.
3. If any EU driving is undertaken in a week the driver must observe the EU driving and rest rules on the day concerned and the EU weekly rest requirements.

What Counts as Duty?

Although the only specific limits on duty time occur in the domestic regulations, where the maximum length of the working day (or spreadover) is 16 hours, it is nevertheless important to be able to determine what constitutes being on duty since this may, under both domestic and Community regulations, impinge on daily or weekly rest time.

Duty Time

Obviously time spent on duty by an employee driving a passenger vehicle will count as duty, as will driving by an owner-driver in connection with his business. In addition it should be appreciated that under Community regulations any time spent driving a passenger vehicle within the scope of the regulations (whether or not as part of a driver's employment) counts as driving time and hence also duty.

However, duty also includes any other time spent acting under an employer's specific instructions. An employee will generally not be considered to be on duty during breaks for rest and refreshment if during those breaks he or she has no specific duties or responsibilities to discharge for the employer.

United Kingdom case law has established that duty embraces any activity from which an employer (or self-employed owner-driver) gains a benefit, or where the driver is under the control of the employer. Note that the fact that payment has been made is not conclusive evidence that a driver was on duty — the payment may, for example, be a bonus or overtime.

A driver is considered to be on duty when:

(a) travelling to take over a bus after "signing on"
(b) awaiting allocation of work on the "spare" rota. (The driver will, however, be "off duty" if released early before the end of his or her rostered spell on the "spare", even if paid to the end of that time. This could bring forward the driver's earliest available time for work the following day)
(c) working for a second employer as a driver
(d) double manning
(e) conducting
(f) in charge of the vehicle during "layover" time at a terminus
(g) inspecting or collecting data
(h) working for a second employer for whom no driving is done.

   Note: This applies only on Community journeys and work — see below.)

A driver is off duty when taking a rostered meal or other break of at least 30 minutes within a period of duty.

Two or More Employers

Most of the above guidelines would apply equally to Community regulated journeys and work, but Community law counts *non-driving work* for another employer as impinging on rest limits whereas a driver under the "Domestic" rules is either an employee or self-employed driver (*Pearson v Rutterford et al 1982*).

Exemptions from British Domestic Hours Regulations for Part-time Drivers

Drivers on domestic journeys and work who do not drive for more than four hours per day in any one week do not have to observe any hours rules during that week.

On two working days per week they may drive over four hours and on each of these two days:
- (a) all duties must start and finish within that 24-hour "day"
- (b) driving time must not exceed 10 hours
- (c) working time must not exceed 16 hours
- (d) there must be 10 hours' rest preceding and following each working day
- (e) if one of the days overlaps into a week in which the part time driving exemption does not apply, limits on driving and spreadover must be observed.

Note: The rule is applicable:
- (a) week by week, not day by day
- (0) to hours of work, not records of work.

7 RESPONSIBILITIES OF THE DRIVER

CUSTOMER CARE — UNDERSTANDING AND HELPING PASSENGERS

Passenger Relations

Good driver/passenger relationships are an essential feature of a successful road passenger transport operation. A driver's relationship with the passengers will be good, and their custom will be retained, if he or she provides the *service* which they want (and for which they are paying). Service and servility should not be confused — it is not necessary to be servile to deliver a professional service and keep the passengers happy.

The Driver's Image

Drivers should always be aware that they are generally the first point of contact between the passenger and the operator. Some passengers may have formed an initial impression of the service from the way they were dealt with when making a telephone enquiry or from speaking to an inspector, and certainly other employees have an important customer care role too, but the drivers' role is paramount. Drivers can reinforce the first good impression or repair an initial poor impression and enjoy greater job satisfaction in the process.

Bus drivers are exposed to the public like actors on stage. Their behaviour reflects on the undertaking. Even when drivers are relaxing and talking amongst themselves, they must be careful not to be critical of their supervisors or colleagues within earshot of passengers!

Passengers observe the cleanliness of the vehicle, the way in which it is driven and the driver's timekeeping. A smooth and uneventful ride is not only the mark of a professional driver, it is also excellent for good customer relations as it confirms to passengers that they were wise to entrust their lives to you!

When passengers board a vehicle it is not usually with the express purpose of having a nice ride — it is because they want to arrive at a destination in safety and on time. But the quality of the ride can be either a bonus or a cause for complaint.

The price of arriving safely and on time is the fare which the passenger usually pays to the driver. Where the quality of service is perceived by the passenger to be poor he or she might be critical of the fares being charged.

Interestingly, passengers don't perceive off-the-bus sales of tickets in the same light, which is one good reason for operators promoting them — they can be good for passenger relations!

Not surprisingly, then, many driver/passenger confrontations arise at the farebox, (or when fare payment is being checked by an inspector).

Understanding passengers
To avoid confrontation as far as possible, drivers need to be able to understand their passengers. Many passengers feel insecure when boarding a bus or coach but try to hide their insecurity because no one likes to look foolish in public. This insecurity can arise in many ways:
  (a) they may be afraid of boarding the wrong vehicle and need assurance that they are on the right one
  (b) they may not know the fare to their destination and are afraid to ask the driver because he or she looks unfriendly
  (c) they may be afraid of being late for an appointment or a connection

(d) they may be having difficulty disentangling complex information on signs, bus stop display boards or timetables especially when services are changing
(e) they may have children or elderly persons "in tow"
(f) they may be young, elderly or disabled themselves
(g) bus stations, airports and railway terminals can be confusing places and scenes of hectic activity, and passengers may easily become confused and be in need of your help.

Good passenger care simply involves recognising passenger anxiety, making allowances for irrational passenger behaviour and trying to be helpful and reassuring.

Product knowledge

Drivers must know their product, ie they must know the route, timetables and fare tables, different types of tickets, passes and tokens and connecting services. They should be prepared to be asked questions and to answer them effectively.

Communication

It is the driver's job to communicate with passengers. Whether this is done on an individual basis or collectively (perhaps using a public address system), the rules are the same:
(a) be prepared — drivers must know what they want to say ("Engage mind before opening mouth" is excellent advice which all drivers should understand!)
(b) be calm — driving is a stressful job, even if the passenger is ruffled, this must not affect the driver — it will do no good
(c) be assertive — drivers should not be bossy, just positive, so that there is no misunderstanding about what they are saying. If the fare is more than a passenger thinks it is, for example, the driver should show him the fare table, there is no need to apologise!

(d) be concerned — most drivers show concern when a blind passenger boards their vehicle, yet many drivers fail to recognise the of travel anxiety

(e) be pleasant — a smile is free but can do more to win passengers than all the advice given so far! Enquiry staff are often told by their employers to "smile on the phone". This is because, even though the people at the other end cannot see the smile, they can often pick up the warmth in the voice which accompanies a smile.

When things go wrong

There is little point pretending everything is fine when the passengers can see for themselves that it isn't! If drivers explain difficulties and delays passengers will usually accept the situation and may even be supportive. Drivers should keep passengers informed about what is being done to correct the problem. Passengers do not like being kept in the dark and can very quickly revert to a state of acute travel anxiety and begin to act irrationally.

Dealing with complaints

Because drivers are the initial, and sometimes only, point of contact between passengers and the operator, they must be prepared to receive their share of complaints. Some of these will be justified, others will be genuine but arise out of a misunderstanding or misinformation. A few will be unjustified.

Most, but not all, people find it difficult to complain. If passengers feel that they have a genuine complaint, they want to be reassured that it will be taken seriously. So drivers should always acknowledge complaints and report them using official report forms, when available. Obviously, if they can deal with the matter "on the spot" they should do so but if not, they should offer to pass it on to the person who can deal with it, or give the passenger details of how he can make the complaint formally if he does not wish the driver to do so.

Most passengers will be happy for drivers to take up their complaints for them if they feel that the drivers can be trusted to do so. Of course it goes without saying that in order to deserve and maintain this trust the complaint must then be passed on. So it is a good idea to get a name and address or telephone number so that passengers can be contacted by the operator.

Summary
Drivers are the ambassadors of the company for which they drive. They are in full view of passengers whom they have to keep happy, secure and informed. To a large extent, drivers create their company's image.

CONDUCT OF DRIVERS, PASSENGERS AND OTHERS

Apart from the requirement by employers for their drivers to behave in a proper manner at all times when on duty, the **PSV (Conduct of Drivers, Inspectors, Conductors and Passengers) Regulations 1990** (SI 1990 No. 1020) as amended by SI 2002 No. 1724 (as amended) contain provisions which they are bound to observe.

Drivers must stop their bus as closely as is reasonably practical to the left or nearside of the road when picking up or setting down passengers, and take reasonable precautions for the safety of boarding, travelling or alighting passengers (the latter provisions must also be observed by any conductor carried on the vehicle).

Conductors and passengers must not distract the driver's attention or obscure his vision whilst the vehicle is moving without having reasonable cause.

Drivers, inspectors or conductors must take all reasonable steps to ensure that passengers comply with the regulations. They must give particulars of their employer's name and address to any police constable or person having reasonable grounds for requiring it, and, in the case of the driver, details of his licence.

Smoking

With effect from 1 July 2007, smoking is legally banned on buses and coaches used in the UK. "No Smoking" signs must be displayed in PSVs and drivers are responsible for enforcing the ban on passengers by acting responsibly and reasonably. Any deliberate infringement by passengers should be drawn to the attention of the operator or (if necessary) the police. (See *Removal of Passengers* below.) Failure to enforce the ban could result in a fine against the driver of up to £2500.

Microphones and Two-way Radio Communications

Drivers may not use a microphone or communicate with anyone directly whilst the vehicle is moving except:
  (a) where it is essential to do so in an emergency or to deal with safety matters
  (b) to communicate with a "relevant person" (the operator or an employee of the operator) on an operational matter so long as he can do so without being distracted from driving the vehicle. *This provision permits the use of two-way bus radios*
  (c) to indicate by means of occasional short statements the location of a vehicle when operating a service for hire and reward at separate fares (except an excursion and tour or sightseeing service) so long as he can do so without being distracted from driving the vehicle.

Passengers

In addition to the smoking ban (see above) passengers on PSVs must not:
  (a) unless directed by a driver, inspector or conductor, use any entrance or exit other than for the purpose which is indicated
  (b) impede any boarding or alighting passengers
  (c) endanger the safety of, or cause discomfort to, other passengers
  (d) trail or throw anything from the vehicle

(e) distribute any printed matter which either seeks or gives information or seeks comment, or offer anything for sale, without the operator's permission
(f) give any signal which might be interpreted by the driver as a signal to start the bus or to stop the bus in an emergency
(g) travel in a part of the vehicle not available for carrying passengers
(h) use or play any noisy musical instrument (including a radio, tape recorder, etc) which may annoy other passengers
(i) refuse to leave the vehicle when instructed by the driver, conductor or inspector because:
  (i) the vehicle is full *or*
  (ii) the passenger has caused a nuisance *or*
  (iii) the passenger's condition is offensive to other passengers *or*
  (iv) the passenger's clothing is in such a condition that it might soil the clothing of others or the fittings of the vehicle.
(j) deliberately interfere with the vehicle's fitted equipment.

Animals

Passengers with accompanying animals must comply with the instructions of the driver, conductor or inspector. If requested they must remove the animal from the vehicle.

Such a request must not be made of a disabled person in respect of his or her guide, assistance or hearing dog provided that sufficient suitable space is available for the dog(s) concerned.

Note: Assistance dogs will be identified by the jacket they must wear when they are providing "assistance".

Bulky, Dangerous or Cumbersome Articles

Passengers with such articles must comply with the instructions of the driver, conductor or inspector as regards where on the vehicle these are to be stowed. If requested they must remove the article from the vehicle.

Such articles will include those which:
(a) are bulky or cumbersome
(b) might be annoying to anyone on the vehicle
(c) might cause injury or danger to anyone on the vehicle
(d) might damage the vehicle or the property of a passenger.

Payment of Fares

A fare is defined in the regulations as an amount paid by a passenger which can be calculated by him from a fare table carried on the vehicle.

If requested, a passenger must state the journey he intends to take or is taking, and must pay the full fare for the journey.

Payment must be made either to the driver when boarding a one person operated bus, or on request to the conductor, or the passenger must use appropriate fare collection or ticket cancelling equipment.

The passenger must leave the vehicle when the journey for which the fare has been paid is completed, or pay the fare for any further journey. *The regulations, in specifying the fare (not excess fare) for any further journey, effectively create the offence of overriding.*

It should be noted that some operators have obtained statutory powers which enable them to charge a penalty fare in the event of a passenger failing to pay the correct, or any, fare.

Other operators attempt to achieve the same ends by including in all their fare tables a hefty "standard fare" (in effect a penalty fare) payable in the event of the correct fare for the journey not being paid.

Tickets

Passengers must not use tickets which are defaced, have been altered, issued to someone else and are not transferable, or which are expired. Any such ticket, or one issued in error, must be surrendered to the driver, conductor or inspector if so requested.

Any ticket issued for the journey (including pre-purchased tickets) must be retained by the passenger for the duration of his journey and be made available for inspection by the driver, inspector or conductor.

Removal of Passengers from the Bus or Coach

The driver, inspector or conductor may request the name and address of any passenger who they suspect of contravening the regulations and may remove from the vehicle any passenger who has contravened these regulations or may seek the assistance of a police constable who is then empowered to remove the passenger.

If the passenger refuses to give his or her name and address to the constable or fails to satisfactorily answer questions put to him or her for the purpose of checking his or her name and address, the constable may arrest the passenger without warrant (**Public Passenger Vehicles Act 1981** s.25(2)).

Non compliance with the regulations is an offence for which they may be liable to a fine at or below Level 3 on the standard scale of fines.

The Obligation to Carry Passengers

Operators have a legal obligation to carry all persons who present themselves for carriage in a fit condition at the proper place and time. A driver is not at liberty to refuse, without good reason, to carry any such person who is prepared to pay the fare and for whom there is room on his vehicle. A driver may, however, refuse a drunken, riotous or offensive person likely to cause annoyance or injury to other passengers and indeed would be in breach of his or her duty of care to the passengers were he or she not to do so.

The PSV conduct regulations amended by virtue of the **Discrimination Act 1995 and 2005**, place specific duties on the driver in respect of the carrying of disabled persons on local bus services (including school bus services when separate fares are charged to passengers by the service organiser) when operating the new "compliant" accessible vehicles. These obligations include:

(a) assisting wheelchair-bound passengers to board/alight and occupy a wheelchair space on the vehicle when available, and to operate any equipment provided on the vehicle for this purpose

(b) displaying and illuminating destination and route number indicators correctly

(c) allowing on board any "assistance dog" which is travelling with a disabled person — provided that space is available.

Note: 1. Just because a person or passenger is disabled does not of itself constitute offence or annoyance to other passengers.

2. A "guide" to these extra specific duties and advice on complying with the Acts is available from the Department for Transport Mobility and Inclusion Unit in London. Telephone: 020 7944 6100.

The underlying principle of the Acts is to allow persons with disabilities to enjoy the facilities that are available without being disadvantaged, whether it be cost, time or effort as compared with a non-disabled person.

PSV operators normally apply standard terms and conditions of carriage but if these are so restrictive as to attempt to remove the operator's absolute liability for the safety of the passengers, the **Public Passenger Vehicles Act 1981** provides that they will be unenforceable.

Operators are liable to those passengers with whom they make a contract of carriage for their own negligence and for that of their servants. The contract is made by the passengers when boarding the vehicle, since this action is taken to signify their willingness to pay the fare.

In most cases the existence of a contract of carriage is obvious because the passenger buys a ticket and there is usually a statement such as "Carried subject to terms and conditions of XYZ Bus Co" printed on the ticket.

Of course, some passengers are carried "gratuitously", ie they pay no fare. However, the Courts have held that such gratuitous passengers as pensioners or employees with free passes none the less have a "licence" to be on the vehicle and that the operator's liability under the laws of negligence cannot be any more restrictive than it can under a contract of carriage. (Drivers can be reassured that as employees they are further protected by their employers' compulsory employee liability insurance.)

An operator is liable for the safety of passengers' luggage carried on a PSV, unless the passenger takes charge of it. The driver's duty of care starts when the luggage is handed to him or her and continues until it is retrieved. He or she must allow sufficient time at stops for passenger to claim their luggage, especially where this is stowed in lockers only accessible from outside the vehicle.

Lost Property

Any person finding lost property on a PSV is required by law to hand it to the driver or conductor, or, if this is not practical, to take it to the operator's lost property office (not to the police).

Drivers (or conductors) must where practicable search their vehicles for lost property at the end of each journey and be prepared to return any found article to anyone claiming it, *provided they can be satisfied as to ownership*. No fee (see below) is payable in this case. Otherwise they must hand it in to their employer for safe custody within 24 hours.

Operators have to keep a record of lost property. They can dispose of unclaimed lost property after a statutory period (usually one month but a shorter time for low value articles and perishable goods.) A charge (not exceeding £2) can be made for the return of lost property. Official documents such as passports must be returned to their issuing authority.

Standing Passengers

The normal maximum number of standing passengers on a PSV is eight or ⅓ of the seating capacity of the bus (or lower saloon in the case of a double decker bus). However, smaller or larger numbers are frequently prescribed by certifying officers when a vehicle is given its Certificate of Initial Fitness or Certificate of Conformity and these limits must be observed by drivers. In addition an operator may decide, or agree with staff, to carry a lesser number of standing passengers. The maximum number of seated and standing passengers or the number which the operator is willing to carry must be shown on the inside of the vehicle in letters at least 25mm high, which must also be visible from outside the vehicle.

Standing passengers are not permitted:
(a) on a half deck vehicle
(b) on the top deck or stairs of a double decker bus
(c) on any part of the gangway forward of the driver
(d) on a PSV with 12 or fewer seats for passengers
(e) on a coach.

Seating Capacity

On PSVs with nine or more passenger seats the number of seated passengers must not exceed the seating capacity of the vehicle as marked (see *Standing Passengers* above).

However, in the case of children under 14 years of age, three seated children may count as two passengers. A child whose fourteenth birthday falls in a school term can be counted as a fourteen year old until the end of the school year in August.

The "3 on 2" rule cannot apply on any seats fitted with seat belts.

A child under five years of age not occupying a seat is not counted as a passenger.

Seat Belt Wearing on Buses and Coaches

New EU-wide rules effective from 18 September 2006 require passengers (except children under 14 years of age) and crew (eg courier) to wear the available seatbelts when travelling on buses and coaches. Urban buses, eg those used in built-up areas entirely on 30mph roads or designed and certified to carry standing passengers are exempt from this new ruling.

Note: The requirements for children aged 3–14 years inclusive are still to be defined by the DfT.

The new law requires that passengers must be informed of the legal requirement to wear the seatbelts (where available) whenever they are seated in any part of the vehicle and the vehicle is in motion. The methods of informing the passengers are by:

(a) the driver (where an operator chooses this method) or
(b) the conductor, courier or designated tour leader or
(c) audiovisual means (such as video) or
(d) signs and/or a pictogram prominently displayed at each and every seating position where a seatbelt is avaliable.

Operators failing to provide the necessary notification face possible fines of up to £2500.

ALCOHOL ON COACHES

Alcohol may be sold on buses and coaches provided that the vehicle concerned has been licensed for such purposes and that it is parked.

Alcohol may be consumed on buses and coaches by passengers subject to the operator's discretion and provided the passengers do not infringe the PSV conduct regulations (above). However, it is an offence for alcohol to be carried (even if not consumed) on a PSV travelling to or from a "designated sporting event" (see below). The operator, hirer, or driver are all liable if they knowingly cause or permit this to happen. Police have powers to stop and search a PSV if they think the law is being infringed. Heavy penalties with maximum fines of up to £1000 and possible jail sentences can be imposed.

Designated Sports Grounds and Spring Events

The **Sporting Events (Control of Alcohol) Act 1985** and its associated regulations make it an offence for alcohol to be carried on public service vehicles used principally for carrying passengers for the whole or part of a journey to or from a designated sports ground or sporting event.

The following is a list of such grounds and events.

England and Wales
1. The home grounds of all football clubs which are members of either the English or Welsh Football Associations.
2. Any other ground in England and Wales used by such clubs.
3. Wembley Stadium.
4. Any ground (not covered by 1–3 above) used for any international association football match in England and Wales.
5. Sheilfield Park, Berwick-upon-Tweed.

The designated sporting events concerned are:
   (a) association football matches where at least one of the participating teams is either a full or associate member of the Football League
   (b) international association football matches
   (c) association football matches in the European Cup; the Cup Winners' Cup; or the UEFA Cup
   (d) association football matches which come within the jurisdiction of the Scottish Football Association
   (e) association football matches which take place outside Great Britain where at least one of the participating

teams either represents the English or Welsh Football Associations; or is a full or associate member of the Football League

(f) association football matches outside Great Britain where at least one of the participating teams is a member of the English or Welsh Football Associations competing in the European Cup; the Cup Winners' Cup or the UEFA Cup.

Scotland

The designated sports grounds are:

Allan Park, Cove
Almondvale Stadium, Livingston
Balmoor Stadium, Peterhead
Bayview Park Stadium, Methil
Bellslea Park, Fraserburgh
Borough Briggs, Elgin
Broadwood Stadium, Cumbernauld
Caledonian Stadium, Inverness
Cappielow Park, Greenock
Celtic Park, Glasgow
Central Park, Cowdenbeath
Christie Park, Huntly
Claggan Park, Fort William
Cliftonhill Stadium, Coatbridge
Dens Park Stadium, Dundee
Dudgeon Park, Brora
East End Park, Dunfermline
Easter Road Stadium, Edinburgh
Excelsior Stadium, Airdrie
Falkirk Stadium, Westfield, Falkirk
Fir Hill Stadium, Partick Thistle
Fir Park, Motherwell
Firs Park, Falkirk
Forthbank Stadium, Stirling
Gayfield Park, Arbroath
Glebe Park, Brechin
Grant Park, Lossiemouth
Grant Street Park, Inverness
Harlaw Park, Inverarie
Harmsworth Park, Wick
Ibrox Stadium, Glasgow
Kynoch Park, Keith
Links Park Stadium, Montrose
MacKessack Park, Rothes
McDiarmid Park, Perth
Mosset Park, Forres
New Douglas Park, Hamilton
Ochilview Park, Stenhousemuir, Larbert
Palmerston Park, Dumfries
Pittodrie Stadium, Aberdeen
Princess Royal Park, Banff

Raydale Park, Gretna
Recreation Park, Alloa
Rugby Park, Kilmarnock
St. Mirren Park, Paisley
Somerset Park, Ayr
Stair Park, Stranraer
Stark's Park, Kirkcaldy
Station Park, Forfar
Station Park, Nairn
Strathclyde Homes Stadium, Dumbarton
Tannadice Park, Dundee
Tynecastle Stadium, Edinburgh
Victoria Park, Buckie
Victoria Park, Dingwall

The sporting events concerned are:

1. Association football matches in the Scottish Premier League, Scottish Football League and the Highland Football League.
2. Association football matches in the competition for:
    (a) the Scottish Association Cup
    (b) the Scottish Football League Cup
    (c) the Scottish Association Qualifying Cup (North)
    (d) the UEFA Champions League
    (e) the UEFA Cup Winners' Cup
    (f) the UEFA Cup, or
    (g) the UEFA Inter Toto Cup.
3. International Association football matches in Scotland.
4. Association football matches (not covered by the above) which come within the jurisdiction of the Scottish Football Association Ltd.
5. International Rugby Union football matches.
6. Association football matches outside Great Britain where one of the teams represents:
    (a) the Scottish FA, or
    (b) a club which is a member of either the Scottish Premier League, the Scottish Football League or the Highland Football League.

Note: The above list of grounds is subject to change. Drivers should check details with their employer.

CLEANLINESS AND FITNESS OF VEHICLES

Drivers should ensure that their vehicles are fit for use and clean when in use. In particular, vehicles should be washed whenever there is any danger of windows becoming too dirty for passengers to see out. It is especially important to ensure that the driver's windscreen is clean, the wipers and washers working and the screen wash bottle is topped up. The vehicle should be swept out and seats dusted and vacuumed regularly. Any torn upholstery, worn floor treads or projecting fastenings or trim which could injure a passenger or damage clothing should be reported. PSV examiners have been known to prohibit the use of a PSV where the above points have been neglected.

Finally, the visual appearance of the vehicle, both inside and out is very important, as is the appearance and manner of the driver — this is especially so where competition allows passengers a choice of services. Even where a choice is not available a dirty vehicle or offhand driver and/or conductor can result in passengers seeking other forms of transport which could lead to the service being curtailed or eventually cancelled through lack of revenue.

Note: A daily "walkround" inspection of the visible condition of the vehicle in respect of bodywork, tyres and windows, the functioning of lights, windscreen washers and wipers and a check for oil and water leaks is required and drivers are generally required to carry out these inspections.

FARES

On most local services and some longer distance services the drivers, unless they have conductors, are responsible for collecting fares and, usually, issuing tickets.

On some "flat fare" services passengers insert the correct fare into a glass fronted fare box and the driver simply checks this and operates a lever to desposit the coins in a sealed vault. On other services with graduated fares there are "Exact Fares Please" and "No Change Given" notices, so that drivers do not handle cash.

On the majority of services, however, drivers issue tickets and give change.

Some operators use tickets with pre-printed fare values, but most systems now utilise ticket issuing machines which print the fare value onto blank ticket rolls. Electronic Ticket Machines (ETMs) which store fare values and details of tickets sold onto computer discs or modules (which can then be downloaded to a computer at the depot) are increasingly being used.

Revenue Protection

The driver is responsible for protecting the operator's revenue. In some cases where a service subsidy has been won by tender the agreement may specify that the operator receives operating costs and the revenue goes to the tendering authority (Passenger Transport Executive or County Council). In this case the driver is responsible for a third party's revenue.

Inspections

For the reasons given above the bus may be boarded by an inspector appointed by either the operator or the tendering authority, who will wish to be satisfied not only that passengers are paying the correct fare but also that tickets have been issued properly and the revenue is being properly accounted for.

In other words inspectors are legitimately looking for both passenger and driver fraud and if a driver obstructs an inspector in the execution of that duty it could have the effect of jeopardising the service subsidy agreement on which the driver's job may depend. The operator might also view such obstruction as misconduct and take disciplinary action against the employee(s) concerned.

Waybills

The waybill is an essential accounting document which has to be reconciled with the cash taken by the driver. Depending on the ticketing system used, the driver may be asked to record the opening and closing serial numbers of pre-printed ticket stocks or the opening and closing cash register readings of the ticket machine.

Electronic Ticket Machines (ETMs) record all or most details required on waybills and can automatically print relevant reports instead of waybills.

Data

Operators, and also tendering authorities who have to reimburse operators for concessionary fares taken and journeys made using off-bus purchased tickets, need to collect data relating to passenger journeys.

Some operators ask drivers to record intermediate figures on their waybills at each terminus for this purpose, others rely on data sampling by their inspectors or specially appointed data collectors. Drivers should co-operate with these staff when they board their buses.

Fare Tables

Fare tables usually show the single adult fare between fare stages. Additionally, information on child fares, OAP concessionary fares, and fares for dogs and parcels will be shown. In some cases a fare code is shown so that when there is a fares revision, new tables do not have to be created. Fare tables can also be pre-loaded with some ETMs allowing drivers to reference these on the machine's display.

Typical Fare Table

Service 427
Oldham Town Centre
20	Clarksfield			
40	20	Lees High Street		
55	40	20	St John's Church	
65	55	40	20	Waterhead

Concession child (5–15 incl.) and OAP, 20p
Parcels and dogs — half fare rounded up to nearest 5p

Typical Coded Fare Table

Service 427
Oldham Town Centre
A	Clarksfield			
B	A	Lees High Street		
C	B	A	St John's Church	
D	C	B	A	Waterhead

Concession Child (5–15 incl.) and OAP = E
Parcels and dogs — half fare rounded up to nearest 5p
A = 20p, B = 40p, C = 55p, D = 65p, E = 20p.

Tickets

Most "on-bus" fare collection systems involve the issuing of tickets and it is essential that drivers ensure that passengers receive a ticket whenever they pay a fare. This is a receipt for the passenger and proves entitlement to travel. The issue of a ticket also supplies data to the operator and enables cash takings to be reconciled.

Off-bus ticket sales
Some operators sell season tickets and multi-journey tickets through outlets such as railway stations, post offices and newsagents.

Multi-journey tickets are usually cancelled by cancellators on the vehicles, but in some cases it is the driver's responsibility to do so using a hand punch.

Most off-bus sales are designed to be attractive to passengers by offering a discount on bulk advance purchases of journeys, unlimited travel for a period (week, month or year) on season tickets, interavailability on other operators' services and special off-peak rates. They are also attractive to operators and drivers as cash is paid in advance and not on the bus and this speeds boarding times.

Drivers should familiarise themselves with the availability by time and route of these various pre-purchased tickets.

Stage numbers
It is the drivers' responsibility to change stage numbers on ticket issuing and cancelling machines as the vehicles pass the various stages. Unless they do so inspectors cannot check their vehicles for over-riders. On some electronically monitored bus service systems the stage numbers (or zones) are charged automatically by the ticket machine.

Passes and permits
Many passengers, such as pensioners and scholars (children too old to qualify for child fares but still in full time education) are issued with permits by operators and local authorities indicating their entitlement to concessionary fares either:
 (a) in general
 (b) at specified times
 (c) on certain journeys.
Other passengers, such as some disabled persons, employees of the company and in some areas, pensioners, may have discount fares or free passes.

Drivers should be able to recognise the passes and permits which are valid on their buses, including those valid as a result of reciprical agreements with neighbouring authorities.

Electronic ticket issuing machines
Many operators, including many minibus operators, use electronic ticket issuing machines.

These are speedy and simple to operate. They overcome many of the difficulties described above as follows.

1. They contain a ROM (read only memory) which is programmed to display the fare for any category of passenger between any two stages. The passenger states the destination and the driver enters the boarding/alighting points. The machine prints a correct value ticket.
2. They also contain a module on which details of every transaction are captured. (It may be necessary for this purpose for drivers to issue "nil fare taken" tickets to holders of free passes or season tickets). The module can be loaded by a driver and taken out when he or she leaves the vehicle. This not only obviates the need for completing a waybill, it also captures full passenger data for use by ticket inspectors and the operator. It can be read directly by a mini computer which is then able to analyse the day's takings by driver, route and vehicle.

It is the driver's responsibility to collect this machine (or module if the machine is mounted permanently in the vehicle) and to return these at the end of the duty. This is especially important in view of the high capital cost of the equipment.

Smartcards

With this system of fare collection, passengers carry a credit card sized personal plastic card containing either a magnetic stripe or an embedded microchip. This can act either as an "electronic purse" on which is stored a pre-paid value (like a telephone card) which is "decremented" when wiped through the driver's electronic ticket machine (ETM), a travel entitlement or pass (eg for school children and some OAPs and disabled travellers with free passes), or a debit card on which information is exchanged between the microchip and ETM, sometimes with a contactless system (like the security gates in public libraries) capturing details of journeys taken and payments due. Drivers required to handle these systems will need to be trained to do so, although in most cases they work automatically with minimum driver involvement.

They are intended to speed boarding and improve travel data capture. The systems are in the main cashless, although some are designed to enable drivers to re-charge a smartcard to the value of cash offered.

8 ACCIDENTS AND INSURANCE

ACCIDENTS

One of the requirements outlined in the Highway Code (but never sufficiently appreciated by drivers) is the information that must be given in the event of being involved in a road accident. The following procedure should be adopted as follows.

1. Stop at the scene of the accident.
2. If any persons are injured seek assistance and send for an ambulance and the police.
3. Try to obtain witnesses.
4. If you have been issued with a camera, take photographs of the scene and the position of the vehicles concerned and of their occupants.
5. Exchange particulars with the driver of any other vehicle involved, ie:
   (a) the name and address of the driver
   (b) the owner's name and address if the driver is not the owner
   (c) the registration number of the vehicle, its type and colour
   (d) where there is personal injury the name and address of the relevant insurance company.
6. Record on paper (or the forms provided by your employer or insurance company):
   (a) the area and extent of any damage sustained
   (b) the time the accident occurred
   (c) where the accident occurred, ie:
      (i) the locality
      (ii) the names of streets and roads adjacent
      (iii) the position of the vehicles at the time of the accident

(iv) the visibility and condition of the relevant road surface at the time of the accident.
 (d) your assessment of the cause of the accident (include any information on whether signals were given).

7. Provide a rough sketch to emphasise the general situation.

All drivers obviously hope that they will not be involved in an accident and are therefore content to leave any consideration of this procedure until one occurs.

It is accepted that drivers, experienced or otherwise, may become nervous and excited when involved in an accident. It is essential, however, that the correct information is obtained *at the time of the accident*. (This is why the use of a camera can be extremely important.) Once the involved parties have dispersed the true facts can never be recalled. This is particularly stressed so that drivers appreciate the important role of factual information in negotiation between insurance companies.

When involved in an accident drivers must not admit responsibility for the accident to the other party or to witnesses; they should leave this for the appropriate authorities to decide.

It should be noted, however, that the law requires a driver to stop and report any damage caused to property on or adjacent to the road or injury to certain animals as a result of an accident, to any person having reasonable grounds for requiring such information including details of insurance. If this cannot be done immediately then the police must be informed as soon as possible and in any case within 24 hours of the occurrence.

In the context of the above, *property* means any other vehicle(s), street furniture, ie traffic signs, bollards, etc garden walls, fences, etc and *animal* means horses, asses, mules, cattle, sheep, pigs, goats or dogs.

Failure to stop or to report an accident is an offence and where reporting to the police is concerned this should be done as soon as possible; any delay (within the 24-hour period) may still bring prosecution if it is considered that the accident could have been reported earlier.

Accident Forms

It is customary for insurance companies to issue accident forms and drivers should see that they carry and understand one of these, as it will serve as a useful guide for obtaining the required information at the scene of an accident.

Company Procedures

In addition to the above legal requirements, many companies issue drivers with their own guidance on accident procedures.

The following is a summary of the more common procedures adopted.

The driver's first consideration should be for the safety and convenience of passengers. The driver is responsible for the elements listed below.

1. Ensure that any injured passengers or other road users receive medical attention as soon as possible.
2. If necessary, summon the emergency services or make sure that this is being done.
3. Try to minimise the danger of any further accidents occuring as a result of the presence of his or her own and other vehicles involved on the road, by arranging for a competent person to direct other road traffic.
4. (Where provided) use a camera to record all relevant information regarding the scene of the accident and the position of vehicles and persons concerned at the time (whether injured or not!)
5. Arrange for a "change over vehicle" to be supplied so that uninjured passengers can continue their journey. (This may also be done by arranging for transfer of passengers onto a following service vehicle if there is room).
6. If possible arrange for an inspector or supervisor to attend the scene of the accident to take statements from witnesses.
7. Obtain the names and addresses of any witnesses to the accident, either bystanders or passengers.

Where the vehicle is in radio contact with the operator the above should not present any difficulty. In other cases the driver should try to find a telephone, reversing the charges if necessary.

INSURANCE

Compulsory Cover

It is legally necessary to have insurance cover in accordance with the Traffic Acts "third party" for a PSV operator. The minimum insurance provides cover for personal injury and property damage sustained by third parties and "full" third party includes cover for loss to the operator through fire damage and theft. Upon the issue of a third party policy, a certificate of insurance is also issued, which confirms that the cover conforms to the Acts. This certificate must be produced (upon request) to a police officer, or, if this is not possible, within seven days at any police station.

The **Road Traffic Act 1988** requires that users of motor vehicles are covered against any liability which may occur in respect of death or personal injury to their passengers in the use of the vehicle on the road. All passengers must be covered and no "own risks" agreements are allowed.

Should insurance be required to cover accidental damage to the operator's vehicle, it is necessary to take out a "comprehensive policy" which, apart from covering accidental damage, also embraces third party risks, fire and theft.

The **Public Passenger Vehicles Act 1981** makes an operator absolutely liable for the safety of his or her passengers at all times while on the vehicle.

Production of insurance certificates
Where a driver is required to produce a vehicle insurance certificate at a police station, there is no obligation for the driver to produce it "in person", the legal requirement is satisfied simply if the certificate is produced. The time limit

for producing the document is "within seven days". However, if it cannot be produced within this period a defence is provided in the **Road Traffic Act 1988** (s.165) if it can be shown that it was produced at the police station as soon as possible, or, due to unforeseen circumstances, it was not reasonably practicable to produce the certificate before the day on which proceedings for non-production were started.

Road Safety Act 2006

This Act created new offences of "causing death by driving whilst uninsured, unlicensed or disqualified" and "keeping vehicles that do not meet insurance requirements".

9 DRIVING OFFENCES

DRINK AND DRIVING

Under the provision of the **Road Traffic Act 1988** it is an offence to drive, attempt to drive or be in charge of a motor vehicle, when having consumed alcohol in such quantity that the proportion of breath alcohol concentration exceeds the prescribed limit, ie 35 microgrammes of alcohol in 100 millilitres of breath (which is equivalent to 80 milligrammes of alcohol in 100 millilitres of blood or 107 milligrammes of alcohol in 100 millilitres of urine).

Penalties prescribed are, on summary conviction, a fine not exceeding £5000, or imprisonment for up to six months, or both.

On conviction on indictment a fine or imprisonment of up to two years, or both, can be imposed (the maximum period of imprisonment on indictment for being in charge of a motor vehicle is one year). In addition, licence disqualification is usually imposed.

Breath Tests and Laboratory Tests

A police constable in uniform can require a driver to take a breath test at the road side if:
   (a) the officer has reasonable cause to suspect the driver of having alcohol in his or her body
   (b) the officer has reasonable cause to suspect the driver of having committed a moving traffic offence
   (c) the driver has been involved in an accident.

Failure to take the test, without reasonable cause, renders the driver liable to arrest and prosecution.

If a preliminary test indicates that the driver is over the limit he or she will be required to go to the police station and unless he or she goes voluntarily the driver can be arrested without a warrant.

At the police station the driver may be required to provide two samples of breath for analysis by an electronic breath testing machine (which gives an instant printout of breath alchohol concentrations) or a specimen of blood or urine for laboratory tests.

Failure, without reasonable cause, to provide a specimen of breath, blood or urine renders the driver liable to prosecution and the officer must warn of this prosecution when asking for a specimen.

A statement automatically produced by the breath testing machine, a certificate signed by the police officer that the statement relates to the breath specimen supplied and blood and urine specimens, shall be admissible as evidence in a prosecution.

A blood specimen may only be taken by a medical practitioner and with the driver's consent.

Of any two breath specimens provided the lower must be used, except if the lower specimen shows no more than 50 micro grammes of alcohol in 100 milligrammes of breath the driver has the right to replace the breath test with a blood or urine test.

The driver may be detained at the police station until the breath test indicates that the alcohol level is below the prescribed limit.

There is a statutory defence against being "in charge" of a motor vehicle if a driver can prove that, at the time, circumstances were such that there was no likelihood of him or her driving whilst exceeding the prescribed limits or whilst unfit through drugs.

Where there has been an accident involving injury to a third party, the police have the power to enter any place where a drink/drive suspect may be, using force if necessary, both to breathalyse and to arrest that person.

DISQUALIFICATION

These are offences for which:
   (a) endorsement is compulsory unless there are special reasons
   (b) courts have discretionary powers to disqualify
   (c) if 12 penalty points are accumulated over three years, disqualification will result for at least six months. Once a period of disqualification has been imposed the existing points incurred under the totting-up procedure will be removed from the licence when re-issued to the driver concerned.

Where more than one offence is committed on the same occasion separate points may be incurred for separate offences.

The three-year period is a rolling term, ie it is measured on each occasion from the date the latest offence was committed.

When disqualification is imposed after the total number of points have been awarded the period of disqualification will be:

- *six months*, if there has been no previous disqualification within the three years
- *one year*, if there has been one previous disqualification within the three years
- *two years*, if there has been more than one disqualification within the three years.

Disqualification can still be imposed for a single offence if it is considered to be serious enough and the liability to obligatory disqualification is retained for drinking and driving offences. (Drivers disqualified on conviction for drunken driving are subject to a minimum ban of one year for a first offence and three years for a second conviction for drunken driving within 10 years.)

OFFENCES FOR WHICH PENALTY POINTS ARE AWARDED

Courts may offer offenders the option to undergo training courses to reduce the number of penalty points awarded.

Courts disqualifying a driver for any of the specified offences below may order him or her to undergo another driving test before reissuing the licence.

Offence	No. of points
Contravention of temporary prohibition or restriction	3–6*
Use of special road contrary to scheme or regulations	3–6*
Contravention of pedestrian crossing regulations	3
Not stopping at school crossing	3
Contravention of order relating to street playground	2
Exceeding speed limit	3–6*
Causing death by dangerous driving	(a)
Dangerous driving	(a)
Careless and inconsiderate driving	3–9
Causing death by careless driving when under the influence of drink or drugs	(a)
Driving or attempting to drive when unfit to drive through drink or drugs	(a)
Being in charge of a vehicle when unfit to drive through drink or drugs	10
Being in charge of a mechanically propelled vehicle with excess alcohol in body	10
Failing to provide a specimen for breath test	4
Failing to provide specimen for analysis or laboratory test	(a)(b)
Motor racing and speed trials on public ways	(a)
Leaving vehicles in dangerous positions	3
Failing to comply with traffic directions	3
Failing to comply with traffic signs	3
Using vehicle in dangerous condition, etc	3

Breach of requirements as to brakes, steering gear or tyres	3
Driving otherwise than in accordance with a licence	3–6
Driving with defective eyesight, or refusing an eyesight test	3
Driving after making false declaration as to physical fitness	3–6
Failing to comply with conditions attached to a provisional or full licence	2
Driving following the failure to notify onset of, or deterioration in, relevant or prospective disability	3–6
Driving after refusal of licence or revocation	3–6
Driving while disqualified:	
– where offender was disqualified as under age	2
– where offender was disqualified by order of court	7
Using motor vehicle without insurance	6–8
Failing to stop after accident and give particulars or report accident	5–10
Failure of keeper of vehicle and others to give police information as to identity of driver, etc in the case of certain offences	3
Manslaughter or, in Scotland, culpable homicide	(a)

* 3 if fixed penalty
(a) 3–11 points if under exceptional circumstances disqualification is not imposed
(b) 10 points, depending on circumstances, if disqualification is not imposed.

OFFENCES FOR WHICH FINES ARE IMPOSED

Fines are imposed for the following offences.
1. Obstructing a certifying officer or vehicle examiner from inspecting a PSV, or from entering premises where such vehicles are kept, for the purpose of inspection.
2. Driving a PSV or causing or permitting the vehicle to be driven, in contravention of a prohibition.

3. Contravention of conditions attached to a PSV operator's licence.
4. Failure to exhibit a PSV operator's disc on the vehicle.
5. Failure to inform Traffic Commissioners of any relevant convictions when applying for, or whilst holding an operator's licence or failure to inform Traffic Commissioners of material change in operating conditions of the holder of the operator's licence.
6. Contravention of regulations providing for the control of number of passengers in public service vehicles.
7. Failure to give notice to Traffic Commissioners relating to failure in, damage to or alteration of a public service vehicle or other information relating to the vehicles in the operator's possession.
8. Providing false information about PSVs in licence holder's possession.
9. Making false statements in order to obtain operator's licence, PCV driving entitlement or variations to such a licence or entitlement, Certificates of Initial Fitness, type approval certificates, operator's discs or certificate of professional competence.
10. Contravention of regulations made under the **Public Passenger Vehicles Act 1981**.
11. Failure to give identity of driver of PSV in certain cases.
12. Driving a PSV without a PCV entitlement or employing a driver without such entitlement to drive a PSV.
13. Contravention of regulations as to conduct of drivers, conductors or inspectors of PSVs.
14. Failing to produce driver's licence for endorsement.
15. Contravention of regulations as to conduct of passengers in PSVs.
16. Failure of persons carrying on the business of operating PSVs to keep accounts and records and to make financial and statistical returns.
17. Forging and misusing documents appertaining to certificates of initial fitness, operator's licences and discs, PCV entitlement, type approval certificates, certificate of

professional competence, a certifying officer or PSV examiner authorisation * fine and/or imprisonment.
18. Contravention of prohibition or restrictions of vehicles using roads of certain classes.
19. Contravention of provisions as to use of special road.
20. Contravention of weight limits on bridges.
21. Contravention of pedestrian crossing regulations.
22. Failing to stop at school crossings.
23. Causing death by dangerous driving † imprisonment.
24. Dangerous driving * fine and/or imprisonment.
25. Careless and inconsiderate driving.
26. Driving or attempting to drive when under the influence of drink or drugs * fine and/or imprisonment.
27. Driving or attempting to drive with excess alcohol in breath, blood or urine * fine and/or imprisonment.
28. Being in charge of a motor vehicle when unfit to drive through drink or drugs * fine and/or imprisonment.
29. Being in charge of a motor vehicle with excess alcohol in breath, blood or urine * fine and/or imprisonment.
30. Failing to provide a specimen for analysis or laboratory test:
    (a) where it was required for ascertaining ability to drive or proportion of alcohol at time the person was driving or attempting to drive * fine and/or imprisonment
    (b) in any other case * fine and/or imprisonment.
31. Failing to submit to a breath test.
32. Speeding.
33. Racing on the highway.
34. Failing to heed traffic directions.
35. Leaving vehicle in a dangerous position.
36. Failing to stop after an accident or report the accident.
37. Obstructing a vehicle from being inspected after an accident.
38. Tampering with vehicles.
39. Driving or riding in a motor vehicle and not wearing a seat belt.

40. Driving a motor vehicle with a child in the front not wearing a seat belt.
41. Driving motor vehicle elsewhere than on roads.
42. Prohibition of parking heavy commercial vehicles on verges and footways.
43. Contravention of Construction and Use Regulations by using or causing or permitting the use of a vehicle adapted to carry more than eight passengers in that it is likely to cause danger:
    (a) by its general condition; the number of passengers being carried; or the weight, distribution, packing or adjustment of the load; the condition of the vehicle's brakes, steering-gear, tyres, or any description of weight; or by its unsuitability
    (b) by the vehicle having an insecure load
    (c) in other cases.
44. Using a vehicle without test certificate:
    (a) when adapted to carry more than eight passengers
    (b) in any other cases.
45. Using a vehicle that has been altered but not notified to the authorities.
46. Using a vehicle without certificate showing the type approval requirements applicable to it.
47. Obstructing an examiner from testing vehicle on the road.
48. Failure of owner of defective vehicle to give certificate.
49. Failure of driver of vehicle on roadside test to give particulars of the owner.
50. Obstructing further testing of vehicle after a reasonable time following the issue of a defect certificate.
51. Selling faulty vehicles or trailers or altering them to make them unroadworthy.
52. Selling vehicle or vehicle part without required certificate showing type approval requirements applicable to it.
53. Drawing more than permitted number of trailers.
54. Allowing vehicle to be on the road without proper lighting.

55. Driving without a licence or employing a person to drive without appropriate entitlement.
56. Failure to comply with the conditions of a provisional licence or full licence treated as a provisional licence.
57. Holding driving licence when particulars are incorrect.
58. Driving with defective eyesight.
59. Refusing to submit to eyesight test.
60. Obtaining a driving licence when disqualified.
61. Driving when disqualified * fine and/or imprisonment.
62. Failing to produce licence for endorsement and/or disqualification, etc.
63. Applying for or obtaining a licence without disclosing current endorsements.
64. Failing to produce licence to court making order for interim disqualification to committal for sentence, etc.
65. Failing to produce to court Northern Ireland driving licence.
66. Failing to give or provide evidence of date of birth or sex.
67. Unregistered and unlicensed persons giving driving instructions for payment.
68. Using motor vehicle without third party insurance.
69. Failing to surrender insurance certificate to insurer on cancellation or to advise its loss or destruction.
70. Failing to give information or making false statements on insurance claims.
71. Failing to stop when required by a constable.
72. Failing to produce driving licence to a police constable.
73. Giving false particulars when stopped for careless or dangerous driving.
74. Failure of driver involved in an accident, where injury to a person occurs, to produce evidence of insurance or report accident.
75. Failure of vehicle owner to supply the police with information to verify the requirements of compulsory insurance.
76. Forgery of licences, test certificates, insurance certificates, etc.

77. Producing false evidence or making false declarations in order to obtain excise licence for vehicle requiring test certificate.
78. Making false statements in connection with the remedying of vehicle defects found on roadside tests.
79. Failure to notify the driving licence authorities of onset of, deterioration in, relevant or prospective disability.
80. Making false statements or withholding information to obtain insurance certificates, etc.
81. Issuing false insurance certificates, test certificates, etc.
82. Failure to attend inquiry, give evidence or produce documents.
83. Failing to attend inquiry when so ordered.
84. Failing to attend or produce documents before a Transport Tribunal.
85. Failing to comply with an operator's licence.
86. Failing to keep records as to hours of work, etc.
87. Failing to preserve records.
88. Failing to produce records.
89. Using a vehicle without an excise licence.
90. Failure to exhibit an excise licence.
91. Failure to observe the automatic half-barrier level crossing regulations.
92. Making false entries on tachograph charts: fine and/or imprisonment.
93. Breaching the drivers' hours rules.

REMOVAL OF DISQUALIFICATION

A person who has been disqualified may apply to the clerk of the court which imposed the disqualification for the removal of the disqualification under the following conditions:
    (a) if the disqualification is for less than four years, when two years from the date on which it was imposed have expired

(b) if the disqualification is for less than 10 years but not less than four years, when half the period of disqualification has expired
(c) in any other case, when five years have expired from the date of disqualification.

If the first removal application is refused, others can be made at three monthly intervals.

If disqualification is for two years or less application for the removal of the disqualification cannot be made. However, application to the quarter sessions for a reduction of the period can be made within 14 days of conviction and disqualification.

Courts disqualifying a driver from driving for any of the offences outlined in the above-mentioned schedules may order another driving test to be taken and passed prior to the reissue of the licence. A driving test cannot be ordered for any other road traffic offence.

If prosecuted for any of the offences listed, the driver must:
(a) submit his or her driving licence to the clerk of the court not later than the day before the hearing or
(b) post the licence to the court to be received not later than the day of the hearing or
(c) take the licence to the hearing.

REMOVAL OF ENDORSEMENTS

Endorsements are not removed from a driving licence until four years after conviction. For drinking and other driving offences the endorsements remain for 11 years.

DUAL LIABILITY

Both the driver or owner-driver and the employer are liable if any of the under-mentioned offences is committed:
(a) contravention of an order relating to street playgrounds

(b) contravention of construction and use regulations:
- (i) in a manner likely to cause danger (vehicle overweight, insecure load, etc)
- (ii) by breach of requirements as to brakes, steering gear, tyres
- (iii) by driving whilst unqualified and employing and allowing a person who does not hold a licence to drive the type of motor vehicle in question
- (iv) by the use of a motor vehicle uninsured or unsecured against third party risks.

An employer who permits or causes the vehicle to be used can also be prosecuted. Under the **Road Traffic Act 1988**, a defence can be made if the employer can prove that he or she did not know that the offence had been committed.

10 USE OF VEHICLES ON THE ROAD

SPEED LIMITS

Speed limits are governed by the **Road Traffic Regulation Act 1984** and apply to roads and vehicles. Where these are different, the lower of the two applies.

General speed limits must be observed by all vehicles on the specific stretch of road to which the limit applies.

The maximum permitted speed on dual carriageways and motorways in Great Britain is 70mph and on single carriageway roads 60mph unless lower speed limits are in force for that road, or the vehicle is in a class which restricts it to a lower limit (see below).

Lower speed limits, usually 30mph, but lesser statutory limits can be imposed, apply to all vehicles on *restricted roads* which either have street lights at intervals of not more than 200 yards or are designated as restricted and have "repeater" speed limit signs erected. Where the 30mph limit has been increased or decreased on a specific restricted road this is indicated by appropriate traffic signs.

Mandatory speed limits (which must not be exceeded) at roadworks on motorways are shown as black figures on a white ground enclosed in a red circle, ie the same signs as used on restricted roads to denote speed limits.

Particular Speed Limits For Certain Classes of Vehicle

Class of vehicle	Motor-ways	Dual Carriageways (other than motorways)	Other Roads
1. A passenger vehicle with an unladen weight exceeding 3.05 tonnes or adapted to carry more than eight passengers:			
– not exceeding 12m in overall length	70	60*	50*
– exceeding 12m in overall length and articulated vehicle	60	60*	50*
2. Dual-purpose vehicle if adapted to carry more than eight passengers	70	60*	50*
3. A passenger vehicle, car-derived van or dual-purpose vehicle drawing one trailer	60	60*	50*

* provided the dual carriageway or other road is not subject to a lower limit.

Exemptions From Speed Limits

Vehicles being used for fire brigade, ambulance or police purposes are exempt from speed limits if such limits are likely to hinder the use of the vehicle for the purpose for which it is being used on that occasion.

LONGER VEHICLES

While this handbook assumes that all PSV drivers are appropriately qualified to drive their vehicles, many drivers will be faced with having to drive vehicles of lengths greater than those for vehicles previously driven. PSVs on rigid chassis can now be up to 15 metres in length and these require additional attention — especially to avoid collision by the rear overhang when manoeuvring from bus stops, parking places, etc and in confined spaces — particularly those not designed for vehicles longer than the previous maximum length of 12 metres.

Drivers of these longer vehicles should be on the look-out for signs restricting the operation of long vehicles, which may be erected by Highway Authorities where they consider that such vehicles present a risk to the safety of the public or other road users.

USE OF MOBILE TELEPHONES AND/OR MICROPHONES

A telephone handset must not be held by a driver whilst the vehicle is in motion or even when the vehicle is stationary, if not parked with the engine switched off. Hands-on telephones may be used in an emergency.

"Hands-free" telephone systems may be used provided the attention of the driver is not likely to be distracted and the driver is in full control of the vehicle at all times.

Offences result in roadside fixed penalty fines of £60 and points endorsement on driving licences. If a case is taken to court, disqualification and a fine of up to £2500 could result if found guilty (The **Road Safety Act 2006**).

Note: The use of any type of microphone to provide commentaries whilst driving is forbidden under the PSV Conduct Regulations (see Section 7).

DRIVING ON MOTORWAYS

Motorways are designed for the purpose of permitting motor vehicles to travel at speed with safety, provided that the rules and regulations laid down are strictly obeyed.

Maximum safety will not be assured unless drivers using motorways are experienced in road procedure and lane drill.

Drivers must also be adept in handling vehicles at speed under prevailing conditions, which include "night driving". Treat the following as a code of practice.
1. Observation drill.
2. Mirror drill.
3. Direction indicator drill.
4. Lights drill.

Rules

A driver must not:
- (a) drive anywhere but on the carriageway
- (b) stop on the carriageway
- (c) reverse on the carriageway
- (d) stop on the central reservation
- (e) stop on verges or hard shoulder, except in case of breakdown, accident or other emergency
- (f) walk on the carriageway or central reservation, except in an emergency
- (g) make a "U-turn"
- (h) use the *outer lane* of a three (or more) lane motorway when driving a bus or coach of any weight, which is constructed to carry nine or more passengers. This prohibition applies irrespective of whether the vehicle is fitted with a speed limiter or not
- (i) disobey remote control signals, such as warning signals — Lane Closed, Maximum Advised Speed, and all other flashing amber light signals
- (j) leave the motorway by an entry road.

Conduct on Motorways

1. When joining a motorway (other than at its start) the approach will be from a road on the left (slip road). Give way to traffic already on the motorway, watch for a safe gap in the inside lane traffic, then accelerate so that the vehicle is travelling at roughly the same speed as the traffic on the motorway.
2. Drive at a steady speed within the limits of the vehicle. On wet or icy roads, or in fog keep the speed down.
3. Driving for long distances can cause drowsiness. To help prevent this make sure there is a flow of fresh air in the driving compartment and suck sweets. When drowsiness occurs, turn off at the next exit or, if nearby, pull into a service area for a break.
4. Exercise caution and drive well within the limits.
5. Know the braking and stopping distances (see *Highway Code*).
6. Extend courtesy to other road users.
7. Do not "hog" the second or outer lanes.

HOV Lanes

High Occupancy Vehicle (HOV) lanes are to be found on some motorways. These lanes are reserved for the use of vehicles carrying two or more people — including buses and coaches.

Motorway Signals

Signals are used on many stretches of motorway and these are usually positioned at two-mile intervals on the central reservation and apply to all lanes. Variable message signs are now commonplace and warn of fog, ice, accidents and lane closures. On some very busy stretches overhead gantry signals are used for direction and lane separation information.

When the road ahead is clear the signals in the central reservation/barrier area are blank, but in dangerous conditions amber lights flash and the central panel of the signal will indicate either in figures (which means a temporary speed limit) or symbols (arrows, etc) that a change of lane is necessary, or that the driver must leave the motorway at the next exit, due to an obstruction ahead.

The signals on overhead gantries, which are positioned over each lane, may also show a flashing red light which means that the vehicle must not *continue beyond the signal in that lane*. Similarly, if red lights flash on a slip road it must not be entered.

All signals should be obeyed since they are there to warn against danger ahead even though it may not be visible.

Driving in Fog on Motorways

Before starting any journey in foggy conditions drivers should:
   (a) check that all lights and reflectors are clean and that lights and indicators are working properly
   (b) clean the windscreen and windows and keep them clean by using wipers, windscreen washer and demister.
1. The maintaining of a safe level of speed and safe separation distance are essential.
2. There is an advisory speed of 30mph for driving in fog.
3. Speed should be checked regularly as fog affects judgement of speed and drivers can easily find themselves speeding up without realising it.
4. Fog makes tail-lights seem further away than they really are.
5. Drivers should know the stopping distances of their vehicles and allow for these.
6. Drivers should use *headlights* or front *fog lights* (if fitted) and *rear fog lights*.

Prohibitions

Among the vehicles that may *not* use motorways are:
– vehicles driven by learner drivers
– pedestrian-controlled vehicles
– animal-drawn vehicles

- agricultural tractors, etc taxed at reduced rate
- engineering plant
- vehicles normally subject to a 20mph speed limit.

Breakdowns

1. If the vehicle breaks down get it on to the hard shoulder, if possible, and leave sufficient room for working on the offside. Position a warning triangle well to the rear of the vehicle.
2. If help is needed, use the motorway emergency telephone system to give an appropriate description of the vehicle and position. From the information in the documents carried give details of equipment, components or tyres, etc which may assist the police in correctly advising the breakdown services of the requirements. Before leaving the vehicle with passengers on board, give instructions to passengers not to leave the vehicle and, if possible, identify a suitable adult to take charge of the passengers until you return. For passenger protection purposes, passengers should, if possible, move towards the front of the passenger area of the vehicle until help arrives.
3. The driver should not wander away from the vehicle as the emergency control cannot call back, so if there is any undue delay a further call should be made to the emergency services.

Condition of Vehicles

Vehicle roadworthiness is essential at all times but before setting out on a motorway journey make sure that the following are checked and are in good order, as so many breakdowns and accidents are caused by the neglect of them:
- oil and water levels
- fuel
- fan belt (and spare)
- brakes
- tyres (condition and inflation pressures), spare wheel and jack

- driving mirrors, windscreen wipers and washers
- lights and reflectors
- steering.

PEDESTRIAN CROSSINGS AND BUS LANES

Zebra Crossings

Zebra crossings consist of rows of alternate black and white stripes between two rows of round or square-headed metal studs placed across the road and marked by a yellow globe on a post containing a flashing light (Belisha beacon). In certain circumstances a constant light may be used.

On either the approach side or both sides of the zebra crossing (depending on local requirements), there is a "zebra controlled area" consisting of two or more white broken zig-zag lines, starting from short lines across the road and approaching the crossing, finishing at a dotted line, the give way line, 1m before reaching the row of metal studs edging the actual zebra crossing.

In the zebra controlled area *overtaking is prohibited and vehicles must stop at the give way line.*

Stopping in the controlled area or on the crossing is also prohibited except to allow pedestrians to cross, or in circumstances beyond the driver's control.

Pedestrians must be given the right of way if they are already on a crossing before a vehicle reaches it. On roads divided by a central reservation or a street refuge (island), each half of the road is treated as a separate crossing.

Pelican Crossings

Pelican crossings are controlled by lights and are operated by pedestrians. The difference between conventional three-light signals and the pelican signals is the flashing amber signal which appears immediately after the red as opposed to the red/amber signal. Pedestrians continue to have precedence on a crossing when the amber light is flashing but if no pedestrians are crossing vehicles may proceed.

Zebra crossing style zig-zag markings also apply to pelican crossings and in the controlled area drivers are prohibited from overtaking a vehicle. Also they may not park or stop in the controlled area unless required to do so at the give way line.

Bus Lanes

Bus lanes on general purpose roads are provided for the improved reliability of bus and coach services and it may be an offence for other vehicles to enter these lanes when they are in operation (usually during peak hours). The lanes and permitted vehicles are clearly marked with special signs indicating times of operation.

Lanes marked by signs showing "Local buses" are for PSV use by only vehicles operating local bus services.

Red Routes

A scheme for priority route networks operates in London. Known as "Red Routes", double red lines marked on roads mean that vehicles are prohibited from stopping at any time and on roads painted with single red lines stopping for loading and unloading is only permitted *outside* working hours. Buses may only stop at marked bus stops.

Fixed penalties for illegal parking are higher than on other roads.

PARKING RESTRICTIONS

1. It is an offence to leave a vehicle unattended without stopping the engine and securely applying the handbrake.
2. A vehicle and trailer must not be left on the road in such a position as to cause an obstruction.
3. A trailer must not be left on a road detached from the towing vehicle unless the brake is set on at least one wheel

or it is secured by a chain, chock or other efficient device to prevent the wheel from moving.
4. Vehicles must not be parked opposite another vehicle or a road island.
5. Vehicles must not be parked in a dangerous position, ie on a bridge, on a bend, within the studs of a pedestrian crossing, double white lines and clearways.

The following observations apply mainly to tour coaches and not to drivers of local services where stopping for passengers to alight or board is mainly at recognised bus stops.

Loading and Unloading Hours

These are shown by short yellow lines one foot long painted on the kerb at right angles to the edge of the road and indicate the following:
   (a) *single lines* at *intervals* — loading ban at peak hours (am and pm marked on lamp-post)
   (b) *double lines* at *intervals* — loading ban throughout the day, eg 08.00 to 18.30
   (c) *treble lines* at *intervals* — loading bans for more than the working day, eg 08.00 to midnight.

No Waiting and Parking

These restrictions are indicated by longitudinal yellow lines painted on the edge of the road. They do not prevent the picking up and setting down of passengers. Indeed, many local Acts and Orders permit vehicles to stand in "No waiting" streets for this specific purpose and this is especially so in the case of the growing "hail and ride" urban minibus services.

There are three types of yellow lines:
   (a) the dotted single line which indicates "no waiting" for part of the day
   (b) the solid single yellow line which indicates "no waiting" for the normal working day
   (c) the solid double yellow line which indicates "no waiting" for more than the working day.

Like the kerb signs, the times of these bans will be shown on the lamp-post signs.

Note: 1. In a "No Waiting" street drivers may only stop to pick up and set down.
2. A police officer has the right to move drivers on.

Breakdown and Removal of Vehicles

1. If a vehicle breaks down in a prohibited street and must be left in order to obtain assistance, the police or traffic wardens should be notified.
2. The police are empowered to remove any vehicle which is causing an obstruction, contravening waiting restrictions or left in a dangerous position.

Parking Meters

Parking meters are included with the kerb marking signs which are displayed on discs to indicate the "controlled zone".

Double parking beside parking bays, etc which are already occupied is prohibited.

Traffic Wardens

Traffic wardens are empowered to enforce the legal requirements given below.
1. Compulsory lights or reflectors.
2. Waiting and parking restrictions by use of the fixed penalty system.

Fixed Penalty System

Fixed fines can be imposed without the case being heard in court. This system operates in towns and cities throughout the country.

Tickets may be affixed to the vehicle or handed to the driver. In the case of endorseable offences the latter will apply as, provided the driver agrees to pay the fixed penalty, the driving licence will have to be surrendered for endorsement of the maximum number of penalty points. If the licence already shows an accumulation of penalty points which, with the latest offence, would bring the total to 12 or more then the fixed penalty would not be issued as the driver would be liable to disqualification. In these circumstances a prosecution would normally follow.

Where the driving licence is not immediately available the driver must produce the licence within seven days at a police station for the necessary endorsement to be recorded. A receipt will be issued, valid for two months, which will be acceptable in place of the licence if for any reason the licence is again required to be produced.

Fixed penalties for:
(a) using a vehicle without the required test certificate being in force — £200
(b) using a vehicle while uninsured or unsecured against third party risk — £120
(c) failure of vehicle keeper and others to give the police details of the driver, etc — £60
(d) non-endorsable offences — £30 (but see below)
(e) endorsable offence — £60
(f) parking on a "red route" in Greater London — £60
(g) parking offence in Greater London other than on a "red route" — £40

and are payable within 28 days or as specified in the notice. If payment is not received within the time limit the driver will be presumed guilty and the fixed penalty charge will be increased by fifty per cent as a fine for non-payment.

A driver may either pay the fixed penalty or request a court hearing if he considers the circumstances to be wrong or unfair but in either case he must respond before the deadline otherwise he will be liable for the penalty and fine.

Vehicle Emissions — Fixed Penalties

In addition to the fixed penalty system described above, **The Road Traffic (Vehicle Emissions) (Fixed Penalty) Regulations 1997** (SI 1997 No. 3058) and the **Road Traffic**

(Vehicle Emissions) (Fixed Penalty) (England) Regulations 2002 SI 2002 No. 1808) allow specified local authorities, namely Birmingham, Bristol, Canterbury, Glasgow and Westminster City Councils, Middlesbrough Borough Council and the Council of the City of Swansea and County of Swansea, and any other local authority in England (covered by the latter regulations) designated as an air quality management area, to issue fixed penalties for vehicles exceeding emission limits. These councils may appoint officers or any other persons who have successfully completed an approved training course, to test vehicle exhaust emissions and if the limits, as contained in regulation 61 of the **Road Vehicle (Construction and Use) Regulations 1986** (SI 1986 No. 1078) are exceeded, a fixed penalty notice for £60 may be issued.

The **Road Traffic (Offenders) Act 1988** provides for registered owners of motor vehicles to carry the ultimate responsibility for the payment of certain *fixed penalty* and *excess* parking charges when these have not been settled within the time allowed, ie 28 days. The liabilities relate to fixed penalties for the following:

(a) parking a vehicle on a road during the hours of darkness without lights or reflectors required by law
(b) contravention of waiting, parking, loading and unloading restrictions
(c) non-payment of a parking meter charge
(d) keeping a vehicle on a public road without a current excise licence.

Owner liability also extends to excess charges.

Exceptions to these requirements are:

(a) the registered owner shall not be deemed to be the driver if it is proved that at the relevant time the vehicle was in the possession of some other person without the owner's consent
(b) in the case of hired vehicles (hired for less than six months) the payment of the relevant charges rests with the hirer and not the registered owner.

Whilst the ultimate responsibility for the settlement of unpaid charges rests with the owner, this in no way absolves the actual driver.

The **Transport Act 1988** extended the fixed penalty system to cover other traffic offences, including motorway regulations, speeding, failing to comply with traffic directions and various vehicle defect offences, etc and the complete list is as follows.

1. Leaving a vehicle parked at night without lights or reflectors, as required.
2. Waiting, parking, loading or unloading.
3. Controlled parking zone regulations.
4. Failure to display a current excise licence disc.
5. Making "U" turns in unauthorised places.
6. Lighting offences by moving vehicles.
7. Banned right turns and driving the wrong way in a one-way street.
8. Contravening a traffic regulation order.
9. Breach of experimental traffic order.
10. Breach of experimental traffic scheme regulation in Greater London.
11. Using a vehicle in contravention of a temporary prohibition or restriction of traffic on a road, ie where a road is being repaired, etc.
12. Contravening motorway traffic regulations.
13. Driving a vehicle in contravention of order prohibiting or restricting driving vehicles on certain classes of roads.
14. Breach of pedestrian crossing regulations*.
15. Contravention of a street playground order*.
16. Breach of a parking place order on a road.
17. Breach of a provision of a parking place designation order and other offences committed in relation to it, except failing to pay an excess charge.
18. Contravening a parking place designation order.
19. Breach of a provision of a parking place designation order.
20. Contravention of minimum speed limits.
21. Speeding†.

22. Driving or keeping a vehicle without displaying registration mark or hackney carriage sign.
23. Driving or keeping a vehicle with registration mark or hackney carriage sign obscured.
24. Failure to comply with traffic directions or signs.
25. Leaving vehicle in a dangerous position.
26. Failing to wear a seat belt.
27. Breach of restriction on carrying children in the front of vehicles.
28. Driving a vehicle elsewhere than on the road.
29. Parking a vehicle on the path or verge.
30. Breach of construction and use regulations*‡.
31. Contravention of lighting restrictions on vehicles.
32. Driving without a licence*.
33. Breach of provisional licence conditions†.
34. Failure to stop when required by constable in uniform.
35. Obstruction of highway with vehicle.
36. Using a vehicle without the required test certificate being in force.
37. Using a vehicle whilst uninsured or unsecured against third party risk.
38. Failure of vehicle keeper and others to give the police details of the driver, etc.
39. Using a mobile phone (endorsement is now obligatory).
40. Driving a vehicle without having a clear view of the road ahead.

Note: *Endorsement is obligatory in certain circumstances.
†Endorsement is obligatory.
*‡ This now includes the use of mobile telephones whilst driving — see *Use of Mobile Telephones*.

For most of these offences only police officers will issue fixed penalty tickets; traffic wardens will continue to deal mainly with parking offences.

Police officers will still be able to warn drivers. In appropriate cases a police officer will issue a fixed penalty notice or, in more serious cases, prosecute in the normal way. Once a police officer has issued a fixed penalty notice the driver will have 28 days (or as specified in the notice) to pay. The driver still has the option to contest the offence in court and this is explained clearly on the fixed penalty notice. If the driver does not take either course within 28 days the penalty will be increased by 50% and enforced by the courts as an unpaid fine.

The fixed penalty tickets for the less serious non-endorsable offences are usually white.

The endorsable tickets are yellow and attract a higher penalty. Where a police officer has decided to issue a fixed penalty ticket for an endorsable offence the driver's licence will be required so that the existing number of penalty points can be checked. A ticket will be issued and the driver asked to surrender the licence in return for a receipt which will be valid for two months. If the penalty points for the present offence added to those which may already be on the licence total 12 or more — the level for disqualification — the driver will not be issued with a fixed penalty notice but will be reported for prosecution. A driver who is not carrying a licence will be required to take it to the police station of his or her choice within seven days. If a driver is stopped for an endorsable offence it will therefore be much more convenient if he or she is carrying his or her driving licence.

Penalty points for traffic offences are given under *Offences for Which Penalty Points are Awarded*.

Parking on the Road at Night Without Lights

The **Road Vehicles Lighting Regulations 1989** allow vehicles to be parked on the road at night without lights in the following circumstances.

Motor cars, motorcycles and passenger vehicles adapted to carry not more than *eight* passengers provided that:
   (a) the road is subject to a 30mph speed limit, or less
   (b) no part of the vehicle is within 10m of a road junction
   (c) the vehicle is parked close to the kerb and parallel to it and, except in the case of one-way streets, has its nearside to the kerb.

On all other roads and in other circumstances the obligatory side and rear lights must be switched on.

Passenger vehicles adapted to carry *nine or more* passengers excluding the driver, goods vehicles *exceeding* 1525kg unladen weight and any vehicle to which a trailer is attached, must keep their lights (side lamps) on when parked on the road at night.

When lights are required on a parked vehicle two white lights must be shown at the front and two red lights to the rear.

It is *illegal* to use either a single parking light or a device which switches on only the offside front and rear lamps.

Parking in London

Part II of the **Road Traffic Act 1991** provides that contraventions of orders relating to designated parking places in London will no longer be a criminal offence and provision is made for authorities (Metropolitan Boroughs) to appoint their own parking attendants, "clamp" illegally parked vehicles and to impose penalties (recoverable as civil debts). The Joint Committee of London Authorities appoints Parking Adjudicators to conduct a hearing in disputed cases.

With the increase in the numbers of coaches bringing commuters and tourists into the central area of London each day, congestion is inevitable especially when setting down or picking up passengers and when trying to park. In an effort to alleviate this problem the Confederation of Passenger Transport, with the support of the London Tourist Board, the Metropolitan Police, Westminster City Council and the Department for Transport, has produced a *"Code of Practice for the Operating and Parking of Tourist Coaches in London"*.

The code recognises the importance of tourist coaches in Central London where most of the places of interest are situated and also the problems associated with the need to satisfy passengers and make their visit as pleasant as possible.

Copies of the complete Code of Practice and the London Coach Parking Map (now available in interactive format at *www.tfl.gov.uk/vcs/maps*) are available from the Confederation of Passenger Transport (CPT), Drury House, 34–43 Russell Street, London WC2B 5HA. (Tel: 020 7240 3131. Fax: 020 7240 6565).

Congestion Charging

This type of "traffic management" was introduced in London in 2003. Buses and coaches are exempt from the charge under the London scheme.

Charging vehicles for access to parts of other cities is under consideration, eg Edinburgh. A small-scale scheme was also introduced in Durham in 2003 under which only "local buses" fitted with a specific device are allowed access. Other buses and coaches are denied access and passengers wishing access can be set down at coach drop-off points or coach parks nearby.

ADVICE ON TAKING A PSV OUTSIDE THE UK

The key to trouble-free operation beyond the UK is to be thoroughly prepared and to ensure that the driver, vehicle and passengers all have the correct documentation required. (It is taken for granted that the driver will have maps and will have studied the route for the journey concerned, will understand the road signs and will drive safely in accordance with respective speed limits.)

The documentation and equipment required for taking a PSV abroad are given below. The listing is comprehensive and should be used on each occasion irrespective of whether a particular item is required for a particular country.

Vehicle

- Original registration document
- Original current annual test certificate
- GB plate

- Waybill and Model Control Document (the type required for the journey/countries concerned)
- Insurance document (green card)
- Service Authorisation document (applicable for registered services only)
- Certified Copy of Community Licence
- "Tempo 100" permit (Germany) and vehicle rear "100" marker (where fitted)
- "Vitesse 100" permit (France) and vehicle rear "100" marker (where fitted)
- Emergency triangles
- High visibility jacket
- "School Bus" signs (to be available if required)
- Snow chains (as required in the winter months).

Driver

- Passport* (check for visa requirements for those with non-EC passport).
- National (EC) Driving Licence (EC journeys) and International Driving Permit (non-EC journeys).
- Letter from employer authorising driver to drive the vehicle on the journey concerned.
- Tachograph charts for each day (sufficient for each driver and spares).
- Drivers card for digital tachograph.
- Letter of Attestation from employer (explaining any lack of continuity/gaps in the driver's tachograph records covering the working week(s) prior to the continental journey concerned).
- Fuel cards.
- Currency/credit cards.

Passengers

- Passport (check for UK re-entry visa requirements for non-EC citizens)

> **Note:** In general, the minimum required validity is six months, however some countries require a minimum validity of one year.

- Ferry Passenger List (must show name, sex and indication of age for each passenger intending to travel on a sea crossing).

Appendix

DEFINITIONS

AETR	European Agreement for Transport by Road vehicles
BSOG	Bus Service Operators Grant (which is a name change for Fuel Duty Rebate (FDR))
CPC	Certificate of Professional Competence
DfT	Department for Transport
DVLA	Driver and Vehicle Licensing Agency
DVLC	Driver and Vehicle Licensing Centre
GVW	Gross Vehicle Weight
OFT	Office of Fair Trading
PCV	Passenger Carrying Vehicle (refers to the type of vehicle and defines a class of driving licence authorisation)
PSV	Public Service Vehicle (refers to any passenger carrying vehicle with more than 8 passenger seats which is approved by the Department for Transport as fit for use in the carriage of passengers for hire or reward)
PTE	Passenger Transport Executive
TfL	Transport for London (formerly London Regional Transport (LRT))
TSO	The Stationery Office
ULW	Unladen Weight
VOSA	Vehicle and Operator Services Agency (formerly Vehicle Inspectorate (VI) and Traffic Area Offices)

TERMS

Drop back service
Practice of providing an additional vehicle into the normal vehicle requirements for a bus service, for a short period, in order to allow timetable recovery (departure time reliability) on services affected by traffic delays. This additional vehicle allows the other vehicles on the schedule to take increased layover time by "dropping back" to commence a later scheduled departure "on time" rather than continuing to operate "late" on the earlier scheduled journey

Interworking
Operation of vehicles which are scheduled on a regular basis to provide services by alternating between two or more registered bus services

Layover
Time within a bus schedule (running board) between the end of one journey and the commencement of the next

Roster (or rota)
List and pattern of duties (periods of work or "shifts") to be worked by a group of drivers. Drivers are allocated to a place on the roster (where the work is usually split into weeks) and then they rotate around the roster so that, over a period of time, each driver will work the shifts shown on each line (week) of the roster

Running Boards
Driver instructions about the schedule for the vehicle on that particular working day

Spreadover
A type of duty or "shift" where the "on duty" time is spread in two or more short sections over the day — usually with lengthy breaks or rest periods in-between

Tidal Flow operation	Practice of alternating the direction of priority for traffic according to traffic demand for road space

A note on speeds: the use of mph or kph in any regulation or control requirement on speed depends upon whether the "rule" emanates from UK regulations which express speed in miles per hour (mph) or EU regulations that express speed in kilometres per hour (kph).

INDEX

A

3 for 2 concession 67, 152
abroad *see* overseas driving
accidents 165–8
   accident forms 167
   company procedures 167–8
   failing to stop and report 166–7
   procedure 165–8
accommodation for driver 98
AETR (European Agreement for Transport by Road Vehicles) rules
   drivers' hours 107–8, 133
alcohol
   at sporting events 153–6
   on coaches 153–6
   drunken passengers 149–50
   see also drink and driving
ambulance
   exemption from speed limits 184
   see also emergency and other services' vehicles
animals 147
   assistance dogs 147
annual holiday 105
annual testing *see* vehicle certification, approval, inspection and annual testing
anti-competitive practices 14
antilock braking system 71–2
armed services 115
articulated bus
   cut out 73
   definition 51
   trailers 70
   turning circle 73
assistance dogs 147
auxiliary lamps 75

B

badges 46
   Community Accreditation 80
bank holidays 103
blood specimens 172
blue discs 5

body
- fitness 91–2
- maintenance 100

brakes 70–1
- antilock braking system 71–2
- braking efficiencies 72
- doors and 95
- EU braking regulations 88–9
- fitness 88–9
- main and secondary brakes 71
- parking brake 71
- retarders 71
- testing 88–9
- trailers 69, 70, 71, 72

breakdown and removal of vehicles
- motorway driving 189
- parking restrictions 193

breakdown vehicles 114
breaks from driving 25, 106, 110–11, 116
breath tests 171–2
bulky articles 148

bus
- articulated *see* articulated bus
- definition 51
- large bus 52
- maximum dimensions 54
- maximum laden weight 53–4
- seat belt wearing on 153
- weighing 83

bus lanes 191
Bus Punctuality Improvement Partnerships 9
Bus Punctuality Improvement Plan 9
Bus Service Operators' Grant (BSOG) 13
bus stations 12
bus stops 12

C

car sharing 3–4
caravans
- lighting 77
- *see also* trailers

Certificate of Conformity 80, 88, 152
Certificate of Initial fitness 80, 87, 152
Certificate of Professional Competence (CPC) 35–6
- test 36
- training requirements 35–6

certification *see* vehicle certification, approval, inspection and annual testing
children
   3 for 2 concession 67, 152
   seat belts 66–7, 68, 153
cleanliness of vehicles 142, 157
close-coupled
   definition 52
coach
   definition 52
   roof strength 74
   seat belt wearing on 153
Community Bus 4, 16
   drivers 8
   meaning 8, 16
   registration 8
Community Bus Permits 5, 8, 9, 16
Community Drivers' Hours and Recording Equipment Regulations 2007 113
Community Transport 7, 16
competition 9–10
   anti-competitive practices 14
   drivers' behaviour 10
   law 14
   predatory pricing 14
   quality of service 10
   restrictive practices 14
complaints handling 144–5
concessionary fares 15
conduct
   animals 147
   bulky, dangerous or cumbersome articles 148
   drivers, inspectors and conductors 145
   lost property 151–2
   microphone, use of 146
   motorway driving 186–90
   obligation to carry passengers 149–51
   passengers 146–7
   payment of fares 148
   removal of passengers 149
   smoking 146
   standing passengers 152
   tickets 149
   two-way radio communications 146
conductors
   carriage of 101
congestion charging 200
contract of carriage 150–1

courier seats	98
courtesy coach	3
crew allocation	24–7
daily limits	24–5
driving duties	26
overtime	26
types of duty	27
weekly limits	25–6
crew seats	98
cumbersome articles	148
customer care	
cleanliness of vehicles	142, 157
communication	143–4
complaints handling	144–5
driver's image	141–5, 157
passenger relations	141, 142
product knowledge	143
service	141
understanding passengers	142–3

D

daily driving period	24–5, 110, 116
daily rest period	25, 103, 111, 116, 135
dangerous articles	148
dangerous substances	
carriage of	101
"dead" trips	115–16
defect notice	81, 82
destination notices	13
diabetics	42
Dial a Ride	16
differential running times	24
digital tachograph	130–3
company card	132
control card	132
downloading data	132
Driver's Card	130, 131
enforcement checks	133
fees for cards	133
information storage/access	130–2
print-outs	130
workshop card	132
direction indicators	76
Disability Discrimination Act 1995	150
Disability Discrimination Act 2005	150
disabled passengers	150

assistance dogs	147
Dial a Ride	16
seat belts	68
disqualification	47, 173
removal	180–1

dogs
assistance dogs	147

doors 94–6
automatic re-opening	95–6
brakes and	95
emergency exits	94
handles	94–5
interlocking opening with transmission	95
offences	65
opening devices	94–5
power operated	95, 100
requirements	94–6

see also entrances; exits

double manning	111, 116
drink and driving	171–2
breath tests and laboratory tests	171–2
penalties	171

see also alcohol

Driver's Card *see* digital tachograph

drivers' hours
48-hour week	25, 103, 104, 105
adequate rest	104
AETR rules	107–8, 133
annual holiday	105
armed services	115
bonus payments	109
breaks from driving	25, 106, 110–11, 116
Community regulated journeys	25, 107, 108, 109–13
consecutive daily driving periods	112
continuous driving without a break	134
crew allocation	24–6
daily driving period	24–5, 110, 116
daily rest period	25, 103, 111, 116, 135
"dead" trips	115–16
domestic operations	105, 134–6
continuous driving without a break	134
daily intervals of rest	135
domestic hours limits	134
driving time	134
emergencies	136
legislation	108, 134, 135
maximum daily duty	135
maximum total daily driving time	134

```
    minimum weekly rest .................................................................................. 135-6
    part-time drivers, exemptions for ............................................................ 139
    spreadover ............................................................. 26, 29, 135, 137, 139, 204
double manning ........................................................................................... 111, 116
driving time .................................................................................................. 110, 134
EC Regulation 561/2006 ........................................................... 107, 109-13, 118
    exemptions ................................................................................................ 113-17
EC Regulation 3820/85 ...................................................................................... 107
emergencies ............................................................................................ 112-13, 136
fortnightly driving .................................................................................... 110, 117
fortnightly rest ..................................................................................................... 25
maximum daily duty ......................................................................................... 135
maximum number of consecutive daily driving periods ............................ 112
maximum total daily driving time .................................................................. 134
maximum working week ............................................................................ 25, 105
meal breaks ..................................................................... 22, 23, 26, 27, 28, 29
meaning of "driver" .......................................................................................... 108
mixed driving .......................................................................................... 108, 136-9
    duty ................................................................................................................. 137
    duty time .................................................................................................... 137-8
    part-time drivers, exemptions for ............................................................ 139
    two or more employers .............................................................................. 138
night work .......................................................................................................... 105
occasional workers .................................................................................... 105, 107
offences ........................................................................................................... 108-9
opt-out agreement ...................................................................................... 103, 105
"out of service" journeys .............................................................................. 115-16
overseas driving .............................................................................................. 107-8
overtime ................................................................................................................ 26
part-time drivers .............................................................................................. 105
    exemptions .................................................................................................... 139
periodic checks ................................................................................................... 113
periods of availability ........................................................................ 105, 106, 107
positioning trips ......................................................................................... 115, 116
prohibition on certain payments .................................................................... 109
records ................................................................................................................ 107
    EC Regulation 3821/85 ................................................................................ 109
    exemptions ................................................................................................ 129-30
    service timetable and duty roster .......................................................... 129-30
    tachograph see tachograph
reference period ................................................................................................. 105
rest day working .................................................................................................. 26
rest periods ........................................................................................... 104, 105, 106
self-employed drivers ...................................................................................... 104
spreadover .................................................................... 26, 29, 135, 137, 139, 204
steam-propelled vehicles .................................................................................. 115
summary of regulations ............................................................................... 116-17
total fortnightly driving .......................................................................... 110, 117
```

trade union agreements	25, 27
weekly limits	25–6
weekly rest	103, 105, 112, 135–6
working time	
Directive	103
meaning	106
working time rules	104–6

Drivers' Hours (Passenger and Goods Vehicles) (Modifications) Order 1971 .... 134, 135

driver's image 10, 141–5, 157

driving licences
- badges 46
- categories of PSV entitlement 42
- Certificate of Professional Competence (CPC) 35–6
- classes 37–40
- cost and duration 40
- diabetics 42
- disciplinary powers of Traffic Commissioners 45–6
- disqualification 47, 173
  - removal 180–1
- driving test *see* driving test
- duration 48
- endorsement 48, 173
  - removal 181
- epileptics 42
- grandfather rights 35, 49
- maintenance staff 48–9
- medical standards 42
- minimum age limits 37, 39–40
- minimum ages of drivers 45
- offences 48
- passenger carrying vehicles (PCVs) 43
- PCV driving entitlement 39–48
  - changes 49–52
- penalty points 173, 174–5, 194, 198
- preserved buses 49
- production 40–1, 194
- provisional 37–8
- qualifying 37
- renewal and replacement 40
- Third EU Directive on Driving Licences 36–7
- towing trailers 39
- unified licence 41–2, 48

driving offences *see* offences

driving test 38
- cost 39
- PCV 43–6
  - conduct of test 43

documents required for tests	46
minimum test vehicles	44–5
preparation for test	45–6
Third EU Directive on Driving Licences and	37
drop back service	23–4
definition	204
drunken passengers	149–50
dual liability	181–2
dual-purpose vehicle	
definition	52–3
duplication of services	11, 18
duties	16
crew allocation	24–7
daily limits	25
driving duties	26
overtime	26
roster/rota	17, 29–32
daily duty	17, 27–33
definition	204
length	30
record of drivers' hours	129–30
size	27–9
split duties	30
service timetable	11, 13, 17–20, 129–30
types	27
weekly limits	25–6

E

early running	11, 17
electrical equipment	91
electronic ticket machines (ETMs)	158, 159, 161–2
emergencies	
drivers' hours and	112–13, 136
emergency exits	94
access	96–7
lighting	100
marking	101
obstruction	100
emergency and other services' vehicles	
drivers' hours	115
exemption from speed limits	184
lighting	76–7
sirens etc	60
emissions	61, 90
fixed penalties	194–5
Low Emission Zone (LEZ)	61

noise *see* noise
endorsement 48
   removal 181
entrances 93–4
   lighting 100
   obstruction 95, 100
   see also doors
epileptics 42
European Agreement for Transport by Road Vehicles (AETR) rules
   drivers' hours 107–8, 133
exhaust
   emissions 90
   pipes 91
   silencers 74, 90–1
exits 93–4
   access 96–7
   emergency *see* emergency exits
   lighting 100
   marking 101
   obstruction 95, 96, 100
   see also doors

F

fares 157–65
   concessionary 15
   electronic ticket machines (ETMs) 158, 159, 161–2
   fare tables 13, 159–60
   flat fare 157–8
   graduated fares 158
   off-bus ticket sales 142, 160–1
   overriding 148
   passes 161
   payment 148
   penalty fare 148
   permits *see* permits
   revenue protection 158–9
      data 159
      inspections 158
      waybills 159
   separate fare, meaning 3
   smartcards 162–3
   stage numbers 161
   standard fare 148
   tickets *see* tickets
ferry

journeys involving	111
fines	
fixed penalty system	185, 193–8
offences	175–80
fire extinguishers	99
fire service	115
exemption from speed limits	184
see also emergency and other services' vehicles	
first aid	99–100
first used	
definition	53
fitness of vehicles	87–99, 157
fixed penalty system	185, 193–8
vehicle emissions	194–5
flammable substances	101
flat fare	157–8
flexible bus services	32–3
fog	
motorway driving	188
fog lamps	
front fog lamps	75, 78, 79, 188
rear fog lamps	78, 79, 188
high intensity	75–6
foreign travel *see* overseas driving	
fortnightly driving	110, 117
fortnightly rest	25
free transport	3
frequency changes	24
fuel tank	60, 89–90
filling	100
fuel cut off device	90
maintenance	90
position	89–90
fuel tax rebates	14

G

gangways	
obstruction	100
graduated fares	158
grandfather rights	35, 49
gratuitous passengers	151
green discs	5
group hire	4
guard rails	88, 89, 97
guide dogs	147

H

"Hail and Ride"	12–13
"hands-free" telephones	185
hazard warning lights	77–8
school buses	78, 102
headlamps	75
hearing dogs	147
heavy motor car	
definition	51
height of vehicle, displaying	57
High Occupancy Vehicle (HOV) lanes	187
hired vehicles	
operators' licences	5
holiday	105
horns	60
hours of work *see* drivers' hours	

I

image	
driver's	10, 141–5, 157
inspection of vehicles *see* vehicle certification, approval, inspection and annual testing	
insurance	
car sharing and	4
compulsory cover	168–9
production of certificate	168–9
third party	168
interworking	22
definition	204

L

laboratory tests	171–2
lamps *see* lighting	
large bus	
definition	52
late operation	11
layover	
definition	204
lighting	74–9, 92
auxiliary lamps	75
caravans	77
daylight hours	78
direction indicators	76
dual lighting circuit	92
dual pole switch and	91

emergency and other services' vehicles	76–7
exits and entrances	100
fog lamps *see* fog lamps	
hazard warning lights	77–8, 102
headlamps	75
high intensity rear fog lamps	75–6
internal	92, 100
maintenance	79
parking on the road at night without lights	78, 198–9
requirements	74, 79, 92
restrictions	74–5
reverse lights	77
staircases	92
stationery vehicles at night	78
steps	92–3
stop lights	77
trailer lights	77

limousines

stretched	4

loading and unloading hours 192

local authorities

permits, issue of	5
school buses *see* school buses	
taxi licensing	7

local services 10–14

bus stations	12
bus stops	12
Community Transport	16
competition law	14
compulsory participation notices	15
concessionary fares	15
destination notices	13
duplication	11
faretables	13
fuel tax rebates	14
"Hail and Ride"	12–13
London	10
meaning	10
punctuality and reliability	9
retiming of school journeys	11
route number indicators	13
taxis	13
tendered	15
timetables	13
timings	11
traffic regulation conditions	11–12

London

congestion charging	200

local services	10
London Service Permit	10
Low Emission Zone (LEZ)	61
parking	199–200
Red Routes	191
seat belts for child passengers	67
Transport for London (TFL)	10
longer vehicles	185
lost property	151
Low Emission Zone (LEZ)	61
luggage	148
safety	151
luggage racks	92

M

manufacturer's plates	54–5
markings	101
maximum dimensions of buses and coaches	54
maximum laden weights	
buses	53–4
trailers	69
meal breaks	22, 23, 26, 27, 28, 29
microphones	146, 185
minibus	
definition	52
mirrors	59
non-commercial operations	4
taxi operators	6
minimum age limits	
driving licences	37, 39–40
minimum ages of drivers	45
mirrors	58–9
mobile telephones	185, 197
MOT test	
three year Class IV MOT test	84
motor car	
definition	51
motor vehicle	
definition	51
Motor Vehicles (Construction and Use) Regulations 1986	51–74, 81
Motor Vehicles (Driving Licences) (Large Goods Vehicles and Passenger Carrying Vehicles) Regulations 1990	41
motorway driving	185–9
breakdowns	189
condition of vehicles	189–90
conduct	187

fog	188
High Occupancy Vehicle (HOV) lanes	187
prohibited vehicles	188–9
rules	186
signals	187–8

multi-manning *see* double manning

N

negligence	150, 151
night work	105
"no waiting"	
parking and	192–3
noise	74, 90–1
silencers	74, 90–1
number plates	74, 79

O

obligation to carry passengers	149–51
obstruction	
of driver	100
of entrances, exit and gangways	95, 96, 100
offences	48
alcohol	154
causing death by driving whilst uninsured, unlicensed or disqualified	169
disqualification	48, 173
removal	180–1
doors	65
drink and driving	171–2
drivers' hours	108–9
dual liability	181–2
endorsement	48, 173
removal	181
excess charges	195–6
failing to stop and report accidents	166–7
fines	175–80
keeping vehicles not meeting insurance requirements	169
microphones	185
mobile telephones, use of	185, 197
overriding	148
payment of fares	148
penalty points	173, 174–5, 194, 198
seat belts	153
tachographs	119, 121, 124, 126, 127
Office of Fair Trading (OFT)	14

operators' licences ("O" licences) 3–8
   blue discs 5
   breach of regulations 6
   car sharing 3–4
   Community Bus Permits 5, 8
   conditions 10
   curtailment 6
   free transport 3
   green discs 5
   group hire 4
   hired vehicles 5
   orange discs 5
   permits 7–8
   personnel carriers 3
   restricted licences 5, 6–7
   revocation 6
   separate fare 3
   special restricted licences 5, 7, 9
   standard licences 5–6
   suspension 6
   types of 5–8
orange discs 5
"out of service" journeys 115–16
overriding 148
overseas driving 200–2
   documentation and equipment 200–2
   drivers' hours 107–8
overtime 26
overweight vehicles 54, 83
   TE160 notice 83

P

parking
   on Red Routes 194
parking brake 71
parking meters 193
parking restrictions 191–3
   breakdown and removal of vehicles 193
   congestion charging 200
   excess charges 195
   loading and unloading hours 192
   London 199–200
   "no waiting" 192–3
   parking meters 193
   parking on the road at night without lights 78, 198–9
   traffic wardens 193

Passenger Transport Executives 12
passengers
    animals accompanying 147
    bulky, dangerous or cumbersome articles 148
    communication with 143–4
    complaints handling 144–5
    conduct 146–7
    contract of carriage 150–1
    customer care 141–5
    disabled persons 147, 150
    driver's image 141–5
    drunken or offensive 149–50
    gratuitous passengers 151
    licence to be on vehicle 151
    lost property 151
    luggage 148, 151
    obligation to carry 149–51
    overseas travel 201–2
    payment of fares 148
    relations with 141, 142
    removal 149
    standing 152
    tickets 149
    understanding 142–3
passes 161
payment of fares 148
Pearson v Rutterford et al 1982 138
pedestrian crossings 60, 190–1
pelican crossings 60, 190–1
penalty points 173, 174–5, 194, 198
performing rights 58
permit vehicles 7–8
    drivers 8
permits 7–8, 161
    Community Bus Permits 5, 8, 9, 16
personnel carriers 3
petrol tank *see* fuel tank
police
    inspections 81
    on-the-road tests or inspections 80
    prohibitions 82, 83
police vehicles
    exemption from speed limits 184
    see also emergency and other services' vehicles
positioning trips 115, 116
Post Office 7
power operated doors 95, 100
predatory pricing 14

preserved buses 49
private hire-cars
   pre-booking 13
product knowledge 143
PSV (Conditions of Fitness, Equipment, Use and Certification)
   Regulations 1981 87
PSV (Conduct of Drivers, Inspectors, Conductors and Passengers)
   Regulations 1990 145
public holidays 103
Public Passenger Vehicles Act 1981 .... 4, 149, 150, 168, 176

Q
quality control 9–10

R
R v Charlton et al 1993 111
radio interference suppression 61
radio, use of 146
receiving monitors and videos 58
recertification 80
records *see* drivers' hours
Red Routes 191
   parking on 194
removal of passengers 119
rest day working 26
restricted licences 5, 6–7
restrictive practices 14
retarders 71
retiming of school journeys 11
reverse lights 77
reversing alarms 60
Road Safety Act 2006 .... 169, 185
Road Traffic Act 1988 .... 76, 168, 169, 171, 182
Road Traffic Act 1991 199
Road Traffic (Driver Licences and Information
   Systems) Act 1989 ....
41, 45
Road Traffic (Offenders) Act 1988 195
Road Traffic Regulation Act 1984 183
Road Traffic (Vehicle Emissions) (Fixed Penalty) (England)
   Regulations 2002 194–5
Road Traffic (Vehicle Emissions) (Fixed Penalty)
   Regulations 1997 ....
194
Road Transport (Working Time) Regulations 2005 103
Road Vehicle (Construction and Use) Regulations 1986 .... 87, 195
Road Vehicles Lighting Regulations 1989 .... 91, 198
roof strength 74
roster/rota 17, 29–32

daily duty	17, 27–33
definition	204
length	30
record of drivers' hours	129–30
size	27–9
split duties	30

***Rout v Swallow Hotels* 1992** 3
route number indicators 13
running board 17, 20–4
- definition 204
- differential running times 24
- drop back service 23–4, 204
- frequency changes 24
- interworking 22, 204
- tidal flow operation 22–3

S

safety glass 59
schedules 16–24
- differential running times 24
- drop back service 23–4, 204
- duplicate services 11, 18
- early running 11, 17
- frequency changes 24
- interworking 22, 204
- late operation 11
- retiming of school journeys 11
- running board *see* running board
- service timetable 11, 13, 17–20, 129–30
- tidal flow operation 22–3, 205

school buses 4, 9
- hazard warning lights 78, 102
- seat belts 66–7, 68
- signs 101–2

school contracts 15
school journeys
- retiming of 11

seat belts 65–8
- 3 for 2 concession 67, 152
- anchorage points and 65–6
- children 66–7, 68, 153
- on coaches 153
- disabled adults 68
- maintenance 66
- offences 153
- rear seat belts 66

    wearing 67–8
seating 97–8
    capacity 152
    courier seats 98
    crew seats 98
    driver's seat 98
self-employed drivers 104
separate fare
    meaning 3
service timetable 11, 13, 17–20, 129–30
"shared taxi" 13
signals
    motorway driving 187–8
    signalling driver to stop 99
silencers 74, 90–1
smartcards 162–3
smoke emission 61
smoking 146
Social Security Act 1976 39
"Special Regular" services 114
special restricted licences 5, 7, 9
speed limiters 56
speed limits 183–4
    classes of vehicle 184
    exemptions 184
speedometers 55–6
sporting events
    alcohol and 153–6
Sporting Events (Control of Alcohol) Act 1985 154
spreadover 26, 29, 135, 137, 139
    definition 204
stability 87–8
stage numbers 161
standard licences 5–6
standing passengers 152
steam-propelled vehicles 115
steps 92–3
stop lights 77
stretched limousines 4
suspension 92

T

tachograph 56–7, 118–30
    breaking of seals 125
    chart 122–3
    charts used in evidence 127

completed charts	124, 126
damage to chart	126
digital *see* digital tachograph	
drivers' responsibilities	123–6
EC Regulation 561/2006	118
EC Regulation 3821/85	109, 118, 127
emergencies	113
employers' responsibilities	126
faulty	125
instrument checks	120–2
leaving chart in	128
manual entries	128
mode selection	119, 123, 124, 128
offences	119, 121, 124, 126, 127
plaques	120–1
reminders	127–8
repairs, recalibration and sealing	125–6
six-yearly recalibration	120, 121
tampering with	125
two or more employers	126
two-yearly check	120

taxis

local service	7, 13
pre-booking	13
registration	7, 13
restricted licence	6–7
"shared taxi" sign	13
special restricted licence	7, 9
"touting" for business	13

TE160 notice	83
telephone handsets *see* mobile telephones	
television sets	57–8
tendered services	15
testing of vehicles *see* vehicle certification, approval, inspection and annual testing	
Third EU Directive on Driving Licences	36–7
3 for 2 concession	67, 152
tickets	149, 160–5
contract of carriage	150–1
electronic ticket machines	159, 161–2
off-bus sales	142, 160–1
passes and permits	161
smartcards	162–3
stage numbers	161
tidal flow operation	22–3
definition	205
tilt testing	87–8
timetable *see* schedules	

trade union agreements
- drivers' hours 25, 27
- types of duty 27

Traffic Commissioners 3, 5, 6–7, 10, 45–6
traffic regulation conditions 11
traffic wardens 193
trailers 69–70
- brakes 69, 70, 71, 72
- carriage of passengers 70
- close-coupled 52
- definition 52
- detached trailers 69
- driving licence type 39
- length of tow rope 69
- lighting 77
- maximum laden weights 69
- PSVs drawing trailers 70
- unbraked trailers, markings 69

train
- journeys involving 111

Transport Act 1968 .... 107, 108, 134
Transport Act 1985 .... 14, 16, 87
Transport Act 1988 196
Transport Act 2000 14
Transport for London (TFL) 10
turning circles 72–3
- articulated buses 73
- cut out 72–3

twin wheels 55
two-way radio communications 146
type approval certificate 80
tyres 62–5
- breadth of tread 62
- compact temporary spares 63
- of different types 63–4
- illegal use 62–4
- loads and speed ratings 65
- maintenance 64
- recut tyres 63
- service and supply 64
- tie-bars 63
- tread wear indicators 63

U

unified licence 41–2, 48
urine samples 172

V

vehicle certification, approval, inspection and annual testing 79–85
   annual testing 80, 83, 90
   Certificate of Conformity 80, 88, 152
   Certificate of Initial fitness 80, 87, 152
   defect notice 81, 82
   inspection of PSVs 81–2
   recertification 80
   type approval certificate 80
   vehicle inspections 80–1
   vehicle testing 83–4
   weighing of buses etc 83
Vehicle Operator Services Agency (VOSA) 4
   digital tachograph data 132
   inspections 81
   on-the-road tests or inspections 80
   prohibitions 82, 83
   testing centres 84
   weight checks 54
ventilation 98
vintage vehicles 87
Vocational Training Directive 35
volunteer drivers 8, 16

W

warning devices 57
waybills 159
weekly rest 103, 105, 112, 135–6
weighing of buses 83
   see also overweight vehicles
welfare vehicles 5
windows
   cleanliness 59–60
   safety glass 59
windscreens 99
   cleanliness 59–60
   safety glass 59
   wipers and washers 59–60
working time *see* drivers' hours

Z

zebra crossings 190, 191